PREHISTORI

ITS MOUNDS A

BY

E. O. GORDON

Author of
The Life of Dean Buckland;
St. George, Champion of Christendom,
etc.

WITH APPENDICES

BY THE REV. JOHN GRIFFITH

Author of
Edward II in Glamorgan

**A REPRINT OF 1946 REVISED EDITION BY
COVENANT PUBLISHING COMPANY, BRITAIN**

(ORIGINALLY PUBLISHED IN 1914)

PUBLISHED BY

ARTISAN SALES
P.O. BOX 1497 THOUSAND OAKS
CALIF 91360 U.S.A.

ISBN 0-934666-16-4
Library of Congress catalog card number: 84-72709

1

DEDICATED,

By permission to

SIR MELVILLE AND LADY BEACHCROFT,

The latter the lineal descendant of
Beli Mawr, King of All Britain and Wales, B.C. 132.

First Published . . 1914
Second Edition . . 1925
Third Edition . . . 1932
Fourth Edition (Revised) . 1946

A REPRINT OF 1946 REVISED EDITION

CONTENTS

CHAPTER III

PREHISTORIC LONDON
ITS MOUNDS AND CIRCLES,
RELIGION AND CIVILIZATION;
WITH NOTES ON THEIR SCIENTIFIC APPLICATION
FROM COMPARATIVE ANTIQUITY

"Ammeu Pob Anwybod."
"Everything unknown is doubted."

A Welsh Adage.

CHAPTER I

ON THE RELIGION, RACE, LANGUAGE AND LITERATURE OF PRE-CHRISTIAN BRITAIN

"Out of monuments, names, proverbs, traditions, private records and evidences, fragments of story, passages of books and the like we do save and recover somewhat from the deluge of time."

BACON'S *Advancement of Learning.*

"THE history of a nation is the history of its religion, its attempts to seek after and serve its God," says an old writer. Of no nation or country is this more true than of Great Britain, where from the standing stones of Stennis in Orkney, to the Maen Ambres in Cornwall—the prehistoric remains of open-air sanctuaries,—artificial mounds and scientifically constructed astronomical circles, bear witness to the vigour and vitality of a national religion, which has already passed from the primitive into the metaphysical stage, and embodies abstract ideas, astronomical observations and a high and pure code of morals. From the comparative study of antiquity in Chaldea, Arabia, Persia, and Palestine, we now know this religion to have been Druidism, one of the oldest religions in the world, and in its Asiatic and Semitic form of Buddhism, the religion still of one-half of mankind.

Sayce points out that in Babylon and Persia, as in Britain,

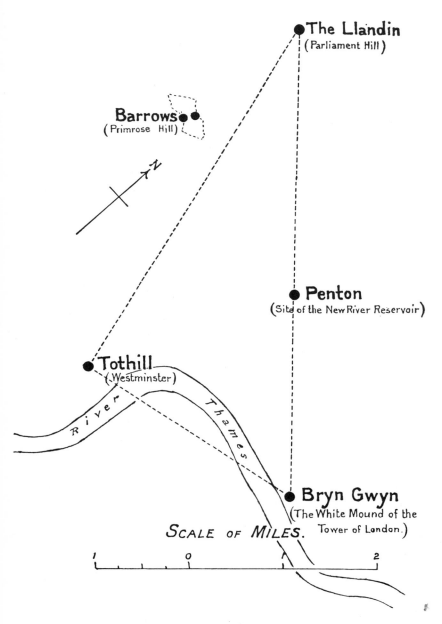

● The Llandin
(Parliament Hill)

Barrows ● ●
(Primrose Hill)

N

● Penton
(Site of the New River Reservoir)

● Tothill
(Westminster)

River

Thames

● Bryn Gwyn
(The White Mound of the
Tower of London.)

SCALE OF MILES.

1   0   2

PLAN OF THE LONDON MOUNDS
(By Stanford)

no ruins of palaces or dwellings are found, magnificent remains of Temples only, witness to the importance the people of these countries attached to their religious worship. Palmer, in his *Desert of the Exodus*, describes prehistoric remains of two kinds in the vicinity of the traditional site of the circle of twelve stones erected by Moses in the Wilderness of Sin (another name for the Moon), huge circles nearly identical with the Druidic circles of our own islands, and, at the head of the valley leading to the Convent on Mount Sinai, he found a small conical mound, called Jebel Moneijah (the Mount of Conference), the prototype probably of our numerous British sacred mounds and places of assembly. Joshua, by God's command, erected a circle at Gilgal (circle) immediately on the Chosen People's arrival in the Promised Land. Stanley describes a circle of stones on the summit of Gerizim, "the Mount of God," which he terms the oldest Sanctuary in Palestine. It was from this circle that Melchisedek, the "Priest of the Most High God," came forth to meet Abraham bearing bread and wine, and it was here that he blessed him and uttered the wonderful promise that has been so literally fulfilled. On the shores of Tyre the Dean points us to a circle as at Stonehenge.

The numerous remains of religious monuments, such as these, in the immediate neighbourhood of the Port of London, afford unmistakable evidence of the large population and great importance of the Capital in remote antiquity.

There is traditional evidence of two Circles, Cors or Courts of Justice, and four conical mounds of unknown antiquity, which like Cathedrals and Churches dominated the moors, marshes and watery stretches that environed the pre-Christian capital. The accompanying diagram, based on the ordnance map, shows the relative position of these prehistoric mounds.

About four miles north-west of St. Paul's towered the largest and most important, the Llandin (llan = sacred, din =eminence, in Welsh signifying a High Place of Worship), Parliament Hill, 322 feet high. About three miles south-east and second in height and size, came the Penton (Pen = head, ton = sacred mound), never known, even at the present day, by other than its Keltic title. "Piled up" on the foreshore of the Thames were the two entirely artificial mounds, the Bryn Gwyn, and the Tothill. On the Bryn Gwyn (Bryn = hill, Gwyn = white or holy), the White Mount, now stands the White Tower of the Tower of London. Two miles west, on Thorn-ey Island, was the Tothill (Tot = a *sacred mound*). It is of interest that Wickliffe, in his translation of the Bible, applies the word "Tot" or "Tote" to Mount Zion (2 Sam. v. 7—9). Not a vestige of the prehistoric mound of the Tothill is now to be seen, but the memory of this ancient "Place of Assembly" survives in the names of Tothill Street and Tothill Fields. That the Mound was standing in Queen Elizabeth's time is certain, from the following mention of it by Norden, the topographer of Westminster, who wrote in this reign, "Tootehill Street, lying in the west part of the cytie, taketh name of a hill near it which is called Toote-hill, in the great feyld near the street." This Hill is marked in Rocques' map (1746) on Toothill Fields, just at the bend in that ancient Causeway, the Horseferry Road. Seventy Rot or Toot Hills are mentioned in Hones' *Year Book*; and many more might be added; he tells us, among the most striking are Tetbury (a corruption of Tot), Teterton Clee and Dod-dington Wood in Salop; the last has a perpendicular height of 122 feet.

To this group of monuments, which must have undoubtedly been the most striking feature of prehistoric London, the derivation of the name (a corruption of Llandin) may be ascribed. Some writers, however, prefer to find the root-word in Llyn, the Welsh for lake; but either derivation is equally descriptive of the surroundings of the Porth (Welsh = the *Gate of the City*) in primitive times. Caer Troia, Troynovant or New Troy, is referred to in several MSS. (other than that of Geoffrey of Monmouth) and by many of the older historians as the name given to London by Brutus the Trojan, the grandson of Aeneas (*circa* 1100 B.C.), the reputed founder of the City. This tradition was never questioned until the last century, when German scholars decided that the story related in Homer's *Iliad* of the siege and destruction of Troy by the Greeks, and subsequent dispersion of the Trojan princes, was a "Poet's dream" and a "mythological myth." The coming of Brutus to Britain was also pronounced to be "fabulous," and a legend that had no foundation in fact.

The following quotation from *Drych y Prifoesedd* ("The Mirror of the Principal Ages"), by the Rev. Theophilus Efans, Vicar of Llangammarch, which has been described as the earliest attempts of modern times to teach their history to the peasantry of Wales, sheds light on the origin of the discredit thrown upon the historical value of Geoffrey of Monmouth's writings. If the statements of Geoffrey of Monmouth stood alone there might be reason for uncertainty, but when we find them frequently corroborated in the old MSS. as well as by Welsh writers of repute, there is no reason to dismiss them as "Monkish fables."

"The first reason for denying the coming of Brutus into this island of Britain was this. When Jeffrey ap Arthur, Lord Bishop of Llandaff (Geoffrey of Monmouth), died, an Englishman of the name of Gwilym Bach (little William or William the Less) arrived, of whom I have already spoken, who desired Dafydd ab Owen, Prince of Gwynedd, to make him bishop in Jeffrey's place about the year 1169 A.D. But when it was not to the mind of Dafydd ab Owen to grant him his request the man went home full of hatred and commenced to exercise his mind how best to despise and malign not only the memory of the bishop, who was lying in his grave, but also the whole of the Welsh nation. This Gwilym Bach, out of malice because he was refused the bishopric of Llandaff, was the first to deny the coming of Brutus here.

"His whole book is nothing else than a tissue of barefaced lies against the Welsh.

"Gwilym Bach says without shame, that no one had ever mentioned the coming of Brutus and his men from Caerdroia to this island until Jeffrey ap Arthur fabricated the tale out of his own imagination, but this is a statement or charge too naked and flimsy without any foundation and against all authority. Because Jeffrey ap Arthur did nothing but translate the Welsh Chronicles into Latin, so that the educated of the country might read them. And long, long before the time of Jeffrey one of the poems (penhillion) of Taliesin makes clear the *consensus* of opinion of his fellow-countrymen in regard to the matter, and he wrote about the year 566 A.D."

Not only do all the Genealogies of the British kings trace

up through Beli the Great, to Aeneas and Dardanus, but this documentary evidence is supported by local tradition at Totnes, and material proof of the landing of the Trojan Prince on our shores, and of his acclamation as sovereign by his kinsfolk from Dartmoor. And as Antiquarians at the present day refer the occupation of this great plateau in Devonshire to a previous colonization in Neolithic times, we get a clue to the possible period of the arrival of the Trojans. Later on, we shall learn the circumstances which led to the departure of Brutus and his companions from their native land, and show from Schliemann and Sayce's discoveries the traces of Trojan influence on the British race and civilization which can neither be disproved nor ignored.

Moreover, Leaf's recently published *Study of Homeric Geography* enables us to see at a glance how remarkably alike in geographical site and surroundings were the historic ports of Troy and Trinovantum or New Troy on the Thames. The Trojan city on the estuary of the Scamander at the mouth of the Dardanelles (the great trade route of the Old World) and London environed by the impregnable marshes and mud flats of the Thames, the great artery leading to the heart of Britain's commerce then as now the life-blood of the nation.

Present day tourists tell us that the principal objects of interest to be seen from the "insignificant Mound of Hissarlik," the ruined site of Troy to-day, are the mounds and tumuli that dot the marshes of the Troad, monuments which are said to date back to the Trojan war and earlier. It may have been the sight of the mounds round about the ancient Caer of London and the tumuli at one time to be seen in the neighbourhood of the Llandin (Parliament Hill) and Primrose Hill, that reminded the exiled Prince of what he must have been told of the ancient glory and commercial importance (as we learn from Leaf) of the famous city of his ancestors, Troy, and suggested to Brutus the name, together with the possibility of founding a New Troy which should rival in brilliance and supremacy the city of his fathers. But as an "alien" and foreign title Caer Troia never became popular with the Britons, or at any time superseded the older name of

Llandin, or London, interwoven as are so many Keltic names, with the highest and noblest of our national ideals.

For certainly it is a striking and inspiring thought, that practically the only traditions that have reached us of the occupation of London in prehistoric times should be those connected with the worship of the "Most High," crystallized in the descriptive titles of the four conical mounds.

By the Welsh, these "high places of worship" are called Gorsedds, a compound of two words, namely, "Gor" and "Sedd," "Gor" signifying "superior," "uppermost," or "supreme," and "Sedd" (dd as "th" in them) "seat." "Therefore 'Gorsedd' means 'supreme seat' and the name is used by the Welsh Britons for the Throne of the Monarch." "It is an institution which belongs exclusively to that parent stem of the Keltic nations called Welsh by the English people, but who call themselves Kymree or Kumri." The term Gorsedd is applied also to the assemblies held either on or around the mound, or within a stone circle, the remains of which circles are often found near the mounds. Maes Howe and the standing stones of Stenness in Orkney, Mass Knoll[1] and Stanton Drew in Somerset are notable examples. On a smaller scale are the remains of a circle at Allington in Kent at the foot of an artificial circular mound on which stands the parish church.

In purely Druidic times, round these "Places of Assembly," all the civil and religious affairs of the district revolved. The Tynwald in the Isle of Man, the artificial mound, the Seat of the Manx Parliament, carries on the continuity of the Druidic Gorseddau or Convocations held at the solstices and equinoxes—"In the face of the Sun, the Eye of Light"—for our forefathers, like the Persians of old, thought it impious to confine the Deity.

In connection with the British Gorsedds of old times, it will be of interest to quote from Cummings' *History of the Isle of Man* the following description of the Annual Assembly held on the Tynwald Hill at the present day, in that it bears so striking a resemblance to the procedure of the Houses of

[1] The site of a British settlement and cemetery.

Parliament in its unique representation of both Church and State, such as exists in no other country:—

"On the Feast of St. John the Baptist, a tent is erected on the summit of the Mound, and preparations are made for the reception of the officers of State, according to ancient custom. Early in the morning the Governor proceeds from Castletown, under a military escort, to St. John's Chapel, which is only a few hundred yards to the Eastward of the Tynwald Hill. Here he is received with all due honour by the Bishop, the Council and the Clergy and the Keys (Representatives of the House of Keys as the local Parliament is still called) and all attend divine service in the Chapel, the Government chaplain officiating. This ended, they march in procession from the Chapel to the Mount, the military forming in line on each side of the Green turf walk. The clergy take the lead, the Juniors being in front and the Bishop in the rear. Next comes the Vicar General and the two Deemsters, then the bearer of the Sword of State, in front of the Governor, who is succeeded by the Clerk of the Rolls, the twenty-four Keys and the Captains of the different parishes. The laws and decisions of the National Council are then proclaimed from the Tynwald Hill—indeed no laws are valid until they have been so proclaimed."

Little less imposing, though in an entirely different way from the London of to-day, must have been the appearance of the primitive city 2,000 or 3,000 years or more B.C. Crowning the cliff of blue clay on the north bank of the Tain or Thames (Keltic = *broad water*) stood the Caer, or fortified enclosure, on precisely the same site as the present city, an area known from time immemorial as the "City Mile"; probably no mile in the world covers more buried history. The Caer consisted of two hillocks, both about 35 feet high, standing on either side of the little stream of the Walbrook which took its rise in the fens beyond Moorgate and flowing through a depression well marked through Lothbury, passed a little to the westward of the Mansion House, and through a kind of ravine to a creek at Dowgate (Keltic = *water-gate*). The present street, called by its name Walbrook, runs very nearly parallel to the course of the stream. The city extended laterally on the east of the present site of the Tower, and on the west as far as the Fleet. To the north lay dreary moorland with fens and swamps stretching to the foot of an immense forest, afterwards known as the Middlesex Forest. Fragments of this primeval forest yet remain at Hampstead (where it is known as Ken or Caen Wood), Highgate,[1] Epping and Hainault.

On the highest ground on the western hillock, where St. Paul's now stands, might have been silhouetted against the sky, the mighty unhewn monoliths of the Druidic circle, the seat of the Arch-Druid of Caer Troia. It is an interesting link with the pre-Christian religion, that St. Paul's has always been the Metropolitan Cathedral of the City of London, a National Church, never at any time a religious corporation ruled by Abbot or Prior.

No trace of the circle remains, but at a little distance to the south-east (originally on the site of the eastern hillock) stands a single obeliscal pillar or index stone, preserved behind iron bars in the wall of St. Swithin's Church, opposite Cannon Street Station. It is said originally to have been a Roman mile-stone, but Sir Lawrence Gomme supposes London Stone, like other great stones, to have marked the place where the open-air assemblies gathered to legislate for the Government of the city. "Some, however, hold this ancient pillar had a yet more ancient destination. In former times this venerable relic was regarded with a sort of superstitious zeal, and, like the Palladium of Troy. the fate and safety of the city was imagined to depend on its preservation" (Brayley).

Index stones, pointers or menhirs are found in connection with many British circles. Perhaps the best known example of a British gnom, pillar or pointer, is the Solitary "Hele" (Gr. Helios = sun) or Sunstone standing somewhat in the same relation to Stonehenge as does London Stone to St. Paul's Churchyard. Another well-known example of an index stone (about 8 feet high) is to be seen, standing 84 yards from the Rollright Circle in Oxfordshire, called to this day the "King Stone." Local tradition associates it with British and Saxon kings. Sixty stones of this circle lie buried in the turf.

---

[1] The "Bishop's Wood," bestowed by the Emperor Constantine on the see of London, and "The Grove," connect Highgate both with the early British Church and with Druidic times.

Dr. Plott inclined to the opinion that here are the remains of a place for the election of a king, but, like most Druidic monuments, their history is enshrouded in mystery.

Stow describes London Stone as "standing in Walbrook, on the south side of this High Street, neere unto the Channell, is pitched upright a great stone called London Stone, fixed in the ground very deep, fastened with bars of iron, and otherwise so stronglie set that if cartes do runne against it through negligence the wheeles be broken, and the stone itself unshaken. The cause why this stone was there set, the verie time when, or other memorie thereof, is there none." London Stone is mentioned as early as the time of Athelstane, King of the West Saxons, without any positive reference to its having been considered a Roman Military stone. We hear of London Stone in the time of Richard II when Jack Cade struck his sword on it. The act was meant to give solemn assurance to the people of his rude fidelity. We have here the survival doubtless of an ancient Druidic form of oath, from a Cornish custom carried out almost to our own day, of business transactions ratified after auction sales at the neighbouring village of St. Buryan, and lovers' troth plighted by the parties concerned shaking hands through a holed stone (now used as a gate post), one of the outlying "pointers" of the Druidic Circle of the Merry Maidens in the Land's End district. The deep-rooted custom seems unmistakably to link Britain with ancient Israel, from the notable example of Laban making covenant with Jacob for the welfare of his daughters and their children by erecting a stone called Galeed, meaning "a heap of witness." In the Biblical record, the stone witnessed both a business agreement and a marriage settlement (Gen. xxxi. 50).

The memory of the Druidic College in London, where lived the Guardians of the Circle, survives in the name of College Street, situated between Dowgate Hill and College Hill, close to Cannon Street Station. Remains have been found hereabouts which were supposed to indicate the site of ancient British dwellings; and on the west bank of the port of the Dowgate traces were discovered of a kind of rude dock for building ships. If *Wal* or *Gael* means foreigners, then the Walbrook may be taken as a reference to the numerous merchants who frequented the narrow waterway, the highway of commerce leading from the broad waters of the Tain into the heart of the city. The exit and entrance of all vessels would probably have been controlled at the Dowgate, by the Druid authorities from the neighbouring College. The Kymric city was as dependent on its shipping for food supplies as is the London of to-day on its railways.

The Druidical Sanctuary or "Place of Refuge," attached to the city circle, became merged, it would appear, in very early times into the Christian Sanctuary of the Collegiate Church of St. Martin-le-grand, which, according to a very ancient tradition, was founded by Cadwallon, a British king. The General Post Office now stands on the site of both Church and Sanctuary. The fact that the privileges of sanctuary survived to the reign of James I, long after the Church and Monastic buildings had perished, is characteristic of the permanence of British Institutions.

About two miles west of the Port of London on Thorney Island was a second Druidic circle, with a College and Sanctuary, where now stands Westminster Abbey. The Isle of Thorns was not then the desolate spot that we have imagined it to be. Excavations, traditions, and history have proved beyond doubt that the Island, half a mile in length and rather less in breadth, was a centre of commerce on the highway of trade from north to south, a stepping-stone lying between a marsh and a tidal river, fordable at low tide. On the west stretched a great marsh which could be waded across, the way marked by stakes; and a causeway of large stones laid in the mud enabled the pack-horses to skirt the swamp of what is now Hyde Park and so gain the north road to Tyburn, so called from the stream of that name, which flowed from Hampstead, across Oxford Street, and through Piccadilly, its two branches forming the delta of Thorney Island on which Westminster Abbey was built. On the south side the river, here broad and shallow, could be forded at low water, conducting the traveller to another low island called Lamb Hythe (Lambeth), probably meaning the place of mud; the memory of this ancient ford survives to this day

15

in the name of the street leading to the river, "Horseferry Road." In the names of Ebury, Chelsea, Battersea and Bermondsey we have practically certain proof that Thorney was one of a cluster of islets (ea or eye signifying an island) in this, the shallowest and widest part of the great waterway.

The surroundings of the Druidic Circle and Sanctuary have been graphically described by Sir Walter Besant. A large population, he writes, were drawn together on Thorney in order to provide for the wants of the continuous stream of travellers which flowed all the year round from the Kent and Surrey districts by the old British road from Dover to London, and who made the ford a halting-place before pursuing their journey north, through the Midlands to Chester and York. Caravans and merchants, with their pack-horses laden with wares to be embarked at Dover—metal, salt, hides and corn—returned with commodities to provide for the wants of the wealthier classes. Thorney was not a fortress or place of strategic importance. It was rather, as regards the permanent population, a collection of Inns and Taverns, a Settlement of Lake-dwellers, who, we may suppose, from remains recently brought to light in the Keltic Lake-dwellings of Glastonbury, were skilful potters, weavers and workers in glass and metal. Thorney, as the first ford on the Thames, was quite as important a station as the port and city itself, demanding the control of the Druidical Order, one of whose duties it was to administer justice.

Before we give a detailed account of the part played by these Places of Assembly in pre-Christian civilization, and relate the traditions which connect the Great Seats of London with the personalities of kings whose names are land-marks in the chronology of the Ancient British Dynasty it will be necessary to glance at the tenets and teaching of a religion, which prompted the erection of such stupendous and enduring monuments. And, if we are to be disabused of the popular notion that the Druidical Circles (symbolic of Eternity), and the serpent-shaped avenues by which many were approached (symbolic of the sun's path through the Zodiac), were dedicated to the worship of the sun and the serpent, we must learn under whose auspices Druidism was established and the evidence that has reached us concerning the National Faith of this Island of the West.

Max Müller, the great Philologist of the University of Oxford in the last century, in the following eloquent passage, traces our word for God to the most ancient language in the world, Sanskrit, and, in a remarkable way, links the primitive religion of Britain with the still older religion of India, and finds the primeval connection between the two nations in a spiritual and tangible belief in the same beneficent Deity.

" . . . Beyond and above the heavenly bodies, which were always changing, was the bright unchanging Deva, the life and light of the Universe. This word has come down along the ages in our word Deity, Divine, Dieu, Deus, and in the Welsh Duw, Jehovah, God. From the root Die, to shine, the adjective Deva has been formed meaning originally 'bright.' Deva came to mean, in process of time, 'God,' because it orignally meant bright. The dictionaries give its meaning as God or Divine. In the old hymns of India the sun was looked upon as a supernatural power, not only the bright Deva, who performs his daily task in the sky, but he is supposed to perform much greater work, as the supreme spirit, the Creator of the world. He who brings life and light to-day is the same who brought life and light on the first of days. As light was the beginning of the day, so light was the beginning of creation, and, if a Creator, then also a ruler of the world. There is," adds Max Muller, "a continuity of thought as there is of sound, between the Deva of the Veda, and the Divinity that shapes our ends. We have in such words as Deva and Deus the actual vestiges of the steps by which our ancestors proceeded from the world of sense to the world beyond the grasp of the senses. The way was traced by Nature herself; or if Nature, too, is but a Deva in disguise, by something greater and higher than Nature. The old road led the ancient Aryans as it leads us still, from the known to the unknown, from Nature to Nature's God."

"Those simple-hearted forefathers of ours," so says Charles Kingsley, "looked round upon the earth and said within themselves:—

" 'Where is the All-father, if All-father there be? Not in this earth, for it will perish too; where is He who abideth for ever?'

"Then they lifted up their eyes and saw, as they thought, beyond sun, and moon, and stars, and all which changes and will change, the clear blue sky, the boundless firmament of

17

Heaven. That never changed: that was always the same; the clouds and storms rolled far below it; and all the bustle of the noisy world, but there the sky was still; as bright and calm as ever. The All-father must be there, unchangeable in the unchanging heavens; bright and pure and boundless like the heavens; and like the heavens, too, silent and far off."

But long before Kingsley, the Greeks had discovered the same truth.

"There shone the mirrored Master-mind,
  There earth, there sky, there ocean He designed;
  The unwearied Sun, the Moon complete round,
  The starry lights that the ethereal convex crowned;
  The Pleiads, Hyads with the Northern Team
  And Great Orion's more refulgent beam:
  To which, around the axle of the sky,
  The Bear, revolving, reveals his golden eye
  And shines exalted on the ethereal plain,
  Nor bathes his blazing forehead in the main."

Homer's "Iliad."

In studying the primitive religion of Britain, we should never lose sight of the fact that the Universe was the Bible of the Ancients, the only revelation of the Deity vouchsafed the Gentile nations; as St. Paul said to the men of Lystra, "He left not Himself without witness, in that He did good, and gave us rain from heaven and fruitful seasons" (Acts xiv. 17). The wonders of nature were to them as "the voice of the All-Father," directing their lives and unfolding to their reverent observation the intimations of the stupendous circle of the universal law on which our earth revolves with sun and stars in the service of the Supreme God. By the movements of the heavenly bodies they ordered their lives, regulated the times and the seasons, the days and the years, fixed religious festivals and all agricultural proceedings.

This sublime study of the "Manuscripts of God" in the early dawn of civilization brought man into direct intercourse with the highest mind and intelligence. Kepler's first outburst on his discovery of the laws of planetary motion was, "I have been permitted to think the thoughts of God." "In good time, the fact of Creation became the analysis of the thoughts of the Creator of the Universe,"—reverently taught the devout Swiss Professor Louis Agassiz, that humble-minded expounder of the mysteries of the Kingdom of nature, in the Science School of Harvard University.

One of the greatest testimonies to the spiritual character of the religion of our forefathers is the fact that no graven image or inscribed stone of any kind has ever been discovered of Pre-Roman origin in Great Britain. Among the relics of the Stone, Bronze, and Iron Ages in the British Antiquities Department of the British Museum, there is no evidence whatever of idolatrous worship, as we find in the Assyrian, Greek and Roman Galleries. Not that the primitive religion is unrepresented, for numerous incense-burners of clay on the shelves witness to the common use of the Divine ordinance of burning incense (symbolic of prayer) in the Druidic religion as in the Patriarchal worship of the Israelites. In the Gold Room are several beautiful examples of gold crescent-shaped breast-plates. A similar shaped breast-plate forms part of the Gorsedd Regalia of to-day, and is worn by the Arch-Druid at every Eisteddfod.

At a meeting of the British Association, 1836, held at Stonehenge, when Geology was still in its infancy, it was pointed out by Dr. Buckland[1] that the Altarstone was of "fire-stone," a statement ridiculed at the time, but many years later proved to be correct by Professor Petrie, who, on the altar-stone being raised, discovered several feet of burnt embers beneath, pointing to the probability that here, as in the outer court of the Tabernacle in the Wilderness, may have been an altar of burnt incense. Many references are made in the old Welsh writings to the sacred Fire. "Not mean was the place appointed for conference before the *perpetual fire*" may be descriptive of Stonehenge; the beautiful poem of "The Chair of Taliesin" commences, "I am he who *keeps up the fire*."

In 1901 a thorough investigation of Stonehenge took place in order to raise the Great Trilithon that had fallen on the last night of the last century. On excavating the base to refix it in cement, stone chippings and some flint hammers were

[1] The first Professor of Geology at the University of Oxford.

OLD ENGRAVING OF STONEHENGE

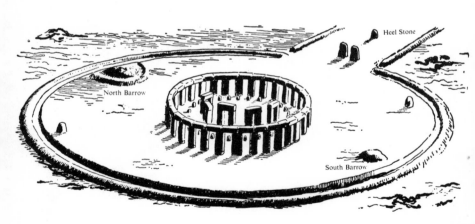

North Barrow

Heel Stone

South Barrow

RECONSTRUCTION OF STONEHENGE

found (now in Devizes Museum) with which it was supposed
the tenons of the Sarsens had been shaped, verifying the
tradition that the Druids used only instruments of flint in
the cuttings for religious purposes to guard against the
making of Idols (Deut. xxvii. 5–6; 1 Kings vi. 7; Joshua viii.
31).

The first Colonizers arrived on our shores "When England
no longer formed part of the Continent, but had assumed its
present physical aspect, its present fauna and flora." This
fact we learn from labels in the cases containing the weapons,
pottery, and personal ornaments of the people who lived in
the Stone, Bronze and Iron Ages, in the British Antiquities
Department of the British Museum. The route of the Kymry
may be traced by the names of the countries through which
they passed, the Crimea and the Chersonese; according to
Dr. Lightfoot, the Galatians retained many traits in common
with the Kymric branch of the Keltic race, and though the
population of Galatia was very mixed, the characteristic
vitality of the Kelts maintained the prominence of the race.
Though Greek became eventually the language of the towns,
the dialect of the country-people was almost identical with
that of the Treveri—the people of Trier or Trèves, founded in
the time of Abraham by Trebeta, the son of Ninus, King of
Assyria, 1300 years before Rome.

But before inquiring into the history of the coming of the
Kymry in the Neolithic or new stone age, it will add to the
interest of our story, first to glance at the remains of the still
older civilization of the Palæolithic or *most ancient stone age,*
when Britain formed part of the continent of Europe, and
elephants, lions, hyenas and bears, roamed the vast forests
which then covered it. In his *Early Man in Britain* Boyd
Dawkins states that the civilization of these River drift and
Cavemen may be compared to that of the Bushmen of Austra-
lia. The great "Ice Age" swept away all traces of the existence
of these Aborigines, except those rude remains that have been
brought to light by the Geologist. Some interesting specimens
of human remains, together with those of wild animals, found
in caves in England and on the Continent, may be seen in the
Geological Gallery of the Natural History Museum in the

wall-case on the right as you enter. Professor Woodward has kindly allowed a photograph to be taken of a specimen of a human skull discovered embedded in the stalagmite floor of a cave. In the centre of the gallery should be noticed the head of a mammoth with tusks 7 feet in length, found at Ilford, a district at one time covered with vast forest, but now a suburb, within half an hour's journey of the city. In pier-case No. 3, near to this old inhabitant of the neighbourhood, is the skull of a British lion, possibly a contemporary of the mammoth.

A map in the British Antiquities Department in the British Museum shows where the footprints of the primitive race have been discovered on the banks of the Thames and other rivers. In the gallery are to be seen specimens of their rough unpolished stone implements, and standing between models of the Druidic circles of Arbor Low, and Stonehenge, is a portion of the floor of a cave-dwelling showing human remains mingled with those of wild animals. No greater contrast could well have been devised that would enable us to realise the low grade of the conditions of life without any religion (so far as we know) and the elevating influence of a knowledge of the True God, the Light and Life of the world. This knowledge inspired the first Colonists to erect their "Bethels" wherever they settled, a consecrated "place of assembly," having no enclosing walls or overarching roof, but a spot set apart for the worship of the Most High, whose Presence the Ancients believed permeated all natural objects.

The footprints of these first settlers have been traced by the remains of their religious monuments (circles and mounds), from the district north of the Persian Gulf, along the trade route of the Phoenicians, to the shores of the Mediterranean. These material remains, when taken in connection with a remarkable affinity in language, the discoveries of modern travellers and the testimony of national traditions, proof that the original Colonists came from Accad,[1] or Accadia, the Southern Province of Babylonia. They brought with them their primitive religion,—"the first wave of the Aryan family to overspread Europe before Greeks or Romans were heard of."

[1] Akkad was one of the four great cities of the land of Shinar.

The earliest recorded history of the British race takes us to Central Asia, the fertile district watered by the Tigris and Euphrates, lying between Mount Ararat on the north and the Persian Gulf on the south. To this country of the ancient Chaldees the earliest settlers in Britain trace their origin.

The Kymry or Kimbri are the Welsh branch of the ancient Keltic people. National traditions maintain that the Kymry possessed from the earliest period of their existence a knowledge of the true God, and embodied it into their theological code as one of the fundamental doctrines of Druidism.

This Keltic literature consists of "The Historic Triads of the Island of Britain," three hundred in number (of which only one hundred and sixty are extant), Bardic Poems, and various fragments of Druidic Philosophy. Like the Sacred Vedas of India the Triads were handed down by oral tradition. Not until the sixth century were they written down by the Bards of King Arthur's Court, Taliesin and Llywarch Hen, when the British king re-organized the "Old Order" on Christian lines and drew up his rules of the Round Table on the Druidic principles of patriotism and self-sacrifice in the cause of King and Country.

In the national Triads of Wales, which are, according to Matthew Arnold and Max Müller, the "oldest literature in the oldest living language in Europe," the eastern origin of the British race is stated:

> "A numerous race, fierce they were called,
> First colonized thee, Britain, chief of Islea,
> Men of the country of Asia, the country of Gafiis.
> Said to have been a skilful people, but the district is unknown
> Which was mother to these warlike adventurers on the sea,
> Clad in their long dress, who could equal them?
> Their skill is celebrated, they were the dread of Europe."

It is not known exactly where Gafis is, but from Layard's discoveries, and Sayce's reading of the clay tablets from the Babylonian Library where he finds a similar form of Monarchical and Constitutional Government to that in early Britain, there seems every reason for thinking it was in this part of the world.

As we have already mentioned, Sayce points out yet one other bond of union between ancient Chaldea and Britain, in the fact that in Babylonia and Persia, as in Britain, no ruins of palaces or dwellings are found; magnificent remains of Temples, only, testify to the importance the people of these countries attached to their religious worship. It is only in the later civilization of Assyria that we find the grandeur of the palaces far exceeds that of the Temples. At Nineveh the Royal Library was kept in the Palace, and not, as at Babylon, in the Temple. It is of no little interest that the ancient Libraries of the Kings of Babylon and Nineveh are now preserved in the British Museum. From these imperishable records inscribed on clay tablets Sayce has discovered that the "Accadian Law did not differ much from our own." He finds here an ancient form of Monarchical and Constitutional Government similar to that which existed in Britain for many centuries before the Christian Era, an organized rule which in primitive times was shared by no other European country. Precedents and previous decisions seem to have been held in as high esteem as among our own lawyers. The king was the supreme court of appeal, and copies exist of private petitions preferred to him on a variety of matters. Judges were appointed under the king and prisons were established in the towns. An old Babylonian code of moral precepts addressed to princes denounced the ruler "who listens to the evil advice of his courtiers and does not deliver judgment according to the law-book."

Another Code which goes back to the Accadian epoch, 3800 B.C., contains an express enactment for protecting the slave against his master. May not this be the seed of imperishable human thought which, lying dormant for centuries, lived again in the spiritual activities of Wilberforce, Livingstone and Gordon, the three saintly men to whom the world owes the suppression of the slave trade.

The status of women is another link between Accad and our own country. Britain has always been a country where the Salic law is not in force, and the exceptional reverence and honour shown to women in all classes of society in all periods of our history, Sayce traces back to the ancient

24

Accadian law which assigned a position to woman that made her the equal of man: in fact, he tells us, she ranked before her husband in matters relative to the family. An interesting article by Hall Caine appeared in the *Daily Chronicle* (March 14, 1910) on the subject of the "Women's Charter," introduced into Parliament by Sir Charles Maclaren, now Lord Aberconway. In this article he states that by Manx law the woman is to all intents and purposes the equal of the man. "The rights of the family in a man's property are most powerfully expressed in the person of his wife, without whose sanction his estate may not be disposed of by will or deed, and may not be encumbered save subject to her widow rights should she survive him. . . . Thus the co-ownership of the wife with the husband is implied in Manx law down to the present day." Here appears a veritable survival in the Isle of Man of the Ancient British and Accadian Law.

Other signs of kinship between Central Asia and these Islands of the West may be observed on the Nineveh sculptures, now within reach of the humblest student in the British Museum. On one of these marbles from Sennacherib's Palace a triumphal procession is depicted in honour of a victory (not a religious procession). The minstrels carry small harps; these, Sir Henry Layard used to take pleasure in pointing out, were the original of the small Welsh harps used by the Keltic bards from the time that they were first established (1000 B.C.) to the present day. A form of the Scottish bagpipes may also be seen on these Assyrian marbles, together with the original of the British war-chariots peculiar to our island. With 4,000 war-chariots Cassivellaunus repulsed the Romans, 55 B.C. In one of the finest monuments in London on Westminster Bridge, Thorneycroft has represented Boadicea in her war-chariot, which only differs from the Assyrian model by the blades fixed in the wheels.

It has been a wonder to many how the gigantic unhewn rocks, weighing 70 or 80 tons, employed in the construction of the Circles of Abury and Stonehenge, were moved and fixed in their respective positions. The method is made clear when we see here depicted the removal of one of the winged bulls of Sennacherib's palace-gate, by the simple process of

rollers, ropes, unlimited amount of human labour, and a
lever. But there is a most important and significant difference to be noticed between Assyrian marbles and the stones
which form the British circles. Whereas the former are
covered with carving and inscriptions, the megalithic remains
in Britain are uninscribed and unwrought (Exod. xx. 25).

Another link with Assyria is mentioned by the late Dr.
Collins, Bishop of Gibraltar, which tends to confirm the
Eastern origin of our prehistoric forefathers. In October,
1907, when on his long and difficult journey as the bearer of
a letter from the Archbishop of Canterbury to the Catholicus
or Patriarch of the Assyrian Church, he came across a Kurdish
village in the district of Ararat which reminded him of the
numerous hut-circles still existing in all part of Britain, but
more especially in Cornwall. With the latter the Bishop was
evidently acquainted, otherwise he would hardly have made
the following entry in his diary:—

> "The village is like a large burrow or warren, consisting of a
> series of earthen mounds of large size, some with solid roofs that
> can be walked on, others that the owners anxiously warn one
> off. The whole thing strongly suggests the underground dwel-
> lings at Chysauster or Treryn in the Land's End district."

It is, however, only within the last century, that fresh light
has been thrown upon the religion and civilization of Ancient
Britain, from the affinity that has been found to exist between
our own and Eastern languages. Dean Alford and Max Müller
point out that the majority of our words are of Celtic, Phoenician, Hebrew, Arabic and Persian origin, and that many
place-names, rivers more especially, are derived from the
Sanskrit. The name of the river "Avon,"[1] for instance, that
forms the eastern boundary of the vast prehistoric cemetery
on the Wiltshire Downs, comes from the Sanskrit root "Av,"

---

[1] There are no fewer than ten Rivers Avon in Great Britain: (1) Eastern
Avon, Wilts and Hants, to English Channel. (2). Lesser Avon, to Bristol
Channel. (3) Little or Middle Avon, Gloucestershire, to River Severn.
(4). Upper Avon, to River Severn at Tewkesbury. (5). River Avon, Mon-
mouthshire, to River Usk. (6). River Avon, Devon, to English Channel.
(7). River Avon, Banffshire, to River Spey. (8). River Avon, to Firth of
Forth at Grangemouth. (9). River Avon, to River Clyde at Hamilton. (10).
River Avon, Glamorgan, to Bristol Channel.

which signifies "water," "on" being expressive of distinct unity, so "Avon" means literally "a river."

In South Wiltshire we find three rivers, the Wyly, the Nadder and the Ebel, whose names, derived from the Sanskrit, are further convincing proofs of the early Eastern occupation. From the name "Wyly" we have "Wilton," the ancient capital of the County itself. The Welsh word "gwili" means "full of turns—winding," and the root of the word is to be found in "gwy," which signifies a flow or flood. Between Wilton and Salisbury, the Wyly receives the waters of the river Nadder. A natural derivation of the word Nadder would seem to be from the Welsh "Neidr," which means a snake or adder. Philologists derive this word from the Welsh "Nad," a shrill noise, or from "Nad-er," to utter a shrill cry. There is in Sanskrit a remarkable confirmation of the probability of such an etymology, for whilst "Nad" means "to sound," "Nada," its derivation, means "a river." The Ebbe or Ebel is a small river in the south-west part of Wilts. The word would seem probably to be derived from the same Sanskrit root ap, or ab, which is found in the Gothic as "Alwa," and in the obsolete Gaelic as "Abh"; the termination of the second form is probably a diminutive, for El has this force in Welsh. *Crib* means "a summit," "Crib-el" a "Cock's comb," "Coq" means "a short piece of wood," and "Coq-yl," a short, stout piece of wood, i.e., Cudgel. Hence "A-bel" or "Eb-el" would mean a little river.

The following examples, taken from a table in Higgins' *Celtic Druids* show the intimate connection that exists between many Eastern and Western words.

Celtic.	Sanskrit.	Roman.	English.
Dia.	Deva.	Deus.	God.
Aran.	Aram.	Aratum.	Cultivated land.
Mathair.	Matara.	Mater.	A Mother.
Brathair.	Bhratara.	Frater.	A Brother.
Di.	Divos.	Dies.	A day.
Son.	Swana.	Sonus.	Sound.
Ceal.	Cealus.	Coelum.	Heaven.
San-scriobhte.	Sanskrita.	Sanctum.	Holy Writ.
Sacred.	Sacrados.	Scriptum.	

Many Phoenician words survive to this day in the British Navy, as Canon Girdlestone, in his exposition of Ezekiel

xxvii. 27, tells us. Such words as "pilot," "caulk," "old salt," etc., and the astronomical signs that represent the days in the week in our nautical almanack of to-day (drawn up three years ahead of time), are the same as those used by the Phoenician sailors who came from the East to the Cassiterides to buy tin.

From Keltic lore it appears that Hu Gadarn the Mighty was the leader of the first colony of the Kymry into Britain about the time of Abraham. In the Triads he is described as one of the "Three Benefactors of the race of Kymry," one of

COINS OF TYRE, SHOWING PILLARS OF HERCULES
(*British Museum*)

the "Three Primary Sages of his adopted land," one of the "Three Pillars of the Race of the Island of Britain." He is reputed to have established Patriarchal worship wherever he went, a tradition supported by the representation of the Petrae Ambrosae, sometimes called the "Pillars of Hercules," on the coins of the city of Tyre,[1] struck in honour of their founder, Hercules. In Britain, Hu Gadarn was regarded as

[1] See coins in British Museum.

28

the personification of intellect and culture, rather than of physical strength, as in Greece. As a peacemaker he stands paramount, for he promoted agriculture, and it is said of him that he would not have lands by forfeiture and contention, but "of equity and in peace."

In Welsh Archæology, Hu Gadarn is commemorated for "having made poetry the vehicle of memory and record," and to have been the inventor of the Triads: to him also is attributed the introduction of several useful arts, such as that of glass-making, and writing in Ogam characters. That these characters were used in Christian times, we know for a fact by the Ogam and Latin inscriptions on a memorial stone at St. Dogmael's, Whitland, Cardigan, South Wales, to Sir Sagramore, one of King Arthur's Knights of the Round Table. (See Malory's *Morte d'Arthur*.)

The Druidic symbol of the name of the Deity is three rods or pencils of light. Of these three lines, in various conjunctions, was framed the first or Bardic Alphabet. Knowledge and religion cannot be separated. In public transactions the Ogam or Bardic characters were employed: in transactions with foreigners, Bardic or Greek.

Hu Gadarn's successor, Ædd Mawr, B.C. 1000, is the reputed founder of the Druidical Order in Britain. He is said to have found within his dominions three Wise Men, called Plenydd, Alawn, and Gwron, and to them he entrusted the work of organization. They took with them the most able men they could find, whom they divided into three orders, Druids, Bards and Ovates, and allotted to them different offices and duties in the business of the State. The title Druid, in Welsh, "der wydd," is said to be a compound of "dar," superior, and "gwydd," priest or inspector. The Irish "Der," a Druid, is the absolver and remitter of sins. The same root is found in the Persian "duree," a good and holy man, and in the Arabic "dere," a wise man. The number of Druids was regulated by very stringent laws in proportion to population.

The Druidic Order, says Matthew Arnold, is the oldest religious and educational institution in Europe. In Britain the Druidical Order numbered thirty-one chief seats of education—each seat was a Cyfiaith or City, the capital of a tribe. The seats of the three Arch-Druids of Britain were Caer Troia = London; Caer Evroc = York; Caer Leon = Caerleon (Mon.).

The seats of the chief Druids of Britain are many of them the capitals of counties to-day, with but slight change in the original Keltic names, as may be seen from the following list, taken from Morgan's *British Cymry*:—

Caer Caint.	Canterbury.	Caerleon ar Dwy.	Chester.
Caer Wyn.	Winchester.		
Caer Municip.	St. Albans.	Caer Peris.	Porchester.
Caer Sallwg.	Old Sarum.	Caer Don.	Doncaster.
Caer Leil.	Carlisle.	Caer Guorie.	Warwick.
Caer Odor.	Bristol.	Caer Cei.	Chichester.
Caer Llear.	Leicester.	Caer Ceri.	Cirencester.
Caer Urnach.	Wroxeter.	Caer Dur.	Dorchester.
Caer Lleyn.	Lincoln.	Caer Merddyn.	Carmarthen.
Caer Glou.	Gloucester.	Caer Seiont.	Carnarvon.
Caer Meini.	Colchester.	Caer Segont.	Silchester.
Caer Gorangon.	Worcester.	Caer Baddon.	Bath.

Although neither Oxford nor Cambridge are mentioned in the above list, the fact remains, that within the precincts of the Law Courts of both cities a prehistoric Gorsedd mound may be seen, a fact which suggests the probability that our Universities, old as they claim to be, were originally Seats of Druidical learning, such as are known to have existed at Caerleon and Glastonbury. The students of the Druidic Colleges, in different parts of the country, are said to have numbered at times 60,000 souls. Amongst these are included the young nobility of Britain and Gaul.

According to tradition, Oxford was founded by Membricius, who was destroyed by wolves when hunting at Wolvercote, three miles distant; hence its Keltic title was Caer Membre, or the "City of Membricius." It was also known as Caer Bosca (probably from the Greek Bosphorus = Ox-ford). This latter name, possibly, was bestowed upon the city when the Greek philosophers, brought by Brutus to Britain, migrated from their original college at Cricklade (Greek-lade) further up the Tain, and set up their school at the suburb of the "Bel Mont" (from which Beaumont Street takes its name), just outside the old city boundary.

Caesar states the head-quarters of the Druids were in Britain, and that those who aspired to be initiated in the more profound mysteries repaired to the British Islands for instruction. They were the ministers of public worship, the depositories of knowledge, and the guardians of public morality. Young men repaired to the Druids for education. They taught theology; they taught the movement of the stars. They presided in Civil and Criminal Courts, and, as with the Church, their heaviest and most dreaded punishment was excommunication.

The different immunities to which the Druids were entitled were the following: ten acres of land, exemption from personal attendance in war, permission to pass unmolested from one district to another in time of war as well as peace, support and maintenance wherever they were, exemption from land tax and contribution from every plough in the district where they were situated. This, according to Welsh authority, is the origin of glebe and close, from the Welsh *Claes*, a green furrow. A most ancient British law provided for the ministers of religion and teachers of the liberal arts.

The Druids and Bards were trained for twenty years in the accurate repetition of the tenets and moral teaching of their order—for the Druids did not consider it lawful to commit their doctrines to writing, or to communicate them outside their own pale. Max Müller compares the Druidical system of teaching to that of the Brahminical. At the present time the Hindoo priests begin their training at the age of ten and continue it for twenty years. No one but a Druid could offer sacrifices,[1] nor was any candidate admissible to the Order who could not prove his genealogy from free parents for nine generations back. The examinations, preparatory to full initiation into the highest grades of the Bards and Druids, were very severe. Nor could he be ordained until he had passed three examinations, three successive years, before the Druidic College of the tribe. The same method of admission by public examination is practised by the Drudic Orders in Wales at the present time. These barriers to promiscuous

---

[1] The charred remains of oxen and deer were found by Sir R. C. Hoare outside the circles of Abury and Stonehenge. Leland mentions a similar find on the south side of St. Paul's, though whether these were Roman or British it was not possible to tell. No traces of human sacrifices have yet been discovered.

A British Druid

A BRITISH DRUID
DRAWING BY WILLIAM STUKELEY, 1723

admission threw the Order almost entirely into the hands of the *Blaenorion,* or aristocracy, making it literally a "Royal priesthood," kings, princes, and nobles entering largely into its composition. But the primitive Druidic laws, unaffected hitherto by foreign innovations, referred the source of all power to the People in congress with the words, "Trech gwlad, nag arglwydd" (Mightier a state than a lord). It is possible that the origin of the House of Lords may be traced to the Druidic aristocracy or *Blaenorion* of Kymric times.

Wordsworth thus expresses appreciation of the Druidical Order:—

"Yet shall it claim our reverence, that to God,
  Ancient of days! that to the eternal Sire,
  These jealous ministers of law aspire
  As to the one sole fount, whence Wisdom flows,
  Justice and Order."

In Druidism the British nation had a high standard of religion, justice, and patriotism presented to them, and a code of moral teaching which has never ceased to influence national character. All national events were recorded in the Triads, and in matters of history the Welsh Bards have ever been consulted as the faithful chroniclers of their time. The metre of some of the Triads show them to be of unquestionable antiquity, and like the sacred Vedas or Hymns of India, our Keltic aphorisms and verses were handed down by oral tradition. These unwritten Keltic records, again, being regularly recited at the Bardic Assemblies, were retained for centuries in their original purity. It was the Druids' intimate knowledge of nature that caused their predictions and "utterances" to be regarded as oracles of truth.

As the secular side of Druidism bore a rude resemblance to feudalism, so on the religious side there was a similar anticipation of the Mediæval Catholic Church. Pliny's definition perhaps best sets before us the position of the Druids. He speaks of the Order in Brittany as the "Gaulish Magi. The name Magi in the East was most august and venerable. They alone were skilled in Divine Matters and were the Ministers of the Deity." When we hear the Druids spoken of as worshippers of the Sun, Moon and Stars, we are apt to lose sight of the fact that it was by the careful observation of the movements of the heavenly bodies that the Eastern Magi were guided to the cradle of the Saviour and were privileged to be the first to worship the "Star" which should rise out of Jacob (Num. xxiv. 17), "the Sun of Righteousness," which the Prophet Malachi foretold 500 years before, should "rise with healing in His wings." It is probable that the Wise men of the East communicated to their brethren the "Wise men of the West," the astrologers and philosophers of Britain, the joyful tidings of their discovery, and the far-reaching results of their journey to Bethlehem; and to this probably may be traced the ready acceptance of Christianity in all parts of these Western Isles.

We are constantly told that the learning and influence of the Druids has been greatly exaggerated; it will be as well therefore to see what Roman writers have to say about them. By Diogenes Laertes, the Druids have been compared with the Chaldeans of Assyria, the Magi of Persia and the Parsees of India in point of learning and philosophy. Ammianus Marcellinus contrasts them with the Pythagoreans, a testimony which is not only honourable in itself, but is entirely in accordance with the evidence of the Welsh Triads. Lucan, an educated Roman, fifty years after Christ, bears testimony to the Keltic races being not only wiser than their neighbours, but ascribes to them high attainments in intellectual and spiritual things, and a belief in a future existence. "To you only is given," he writes, "the knowledge or ignorance (whichever it be) of the gods and the power of Heaven; your dwelling is in the lone heart of the forest. From you we learn that the bourne of man's ghost is not the pale realm of the monarch below. In another world the spirit survives still— death, if your lore be true, is just the passage to enduring life."

The motto of the Druids, "Y gwir erbyn y Byd," "*The truth against the world*," or "*in oppostiion to the world*," embodies the principle of their ancient faith. It survives to the present day as the motto of the Druidical Order in Wales, a fact which goes far to show that on no vital doctrinal point was there any

antagonism between Druidism and Christianity. A summary
of the principal tenets of Druidism will enable the reader to
compare or contrast them with those of Christianity, into
which eventually the national religion merged under the
patronage of the British kings, Arviragus[1] in the first century,
Lleuver Mawr (the Romanized Lucius) in the second, and
Arthur, of European fame, in the sixth. It is interesting to
observe no less where the primitive Gentile religion differs,
than where it agrees with Divine revelation. The summary
is chiefly drawn from the Bardo-Druidic remains in the
Keltic language.

The Druidic religion was brought into Britain, it is said,
by the Gomeridae, from Babylonia, or the Caucasus, at the
first migration under Hu Gadarn. Its leading principles were
the following:—

The universe is infinite, being the body of the being who
out of himself evolved or created it, and now pervades and
rules it, as the mind of a man does his body. The essence of
this being is pure, mental, light, and therefore he is called
Du-w, Duw (the one without darkness). His real name is an
ineffable mystery, and so also is his nature. To the human
mind, though not in himself, he necessarily represents a
triple aspect in relation to the past, present and future; the
creator as to the past, the saviour or conserver as to the
present, the renovator or re-creator as to the future. In the
re-creator the idea of the destroyer was also involved. This
was the Druidic Trinity, the three aspects of which were
known as Beli, Taran, Esu or Yesu. When Christianity
preached Jesus as God, it preached the most familiar name of
its own deity to Druidism; and in the ancient British tongue
"Jesus" ("Saviour") has never assumed its Greek, Latin or
Hebrew form, but remains the pure Druidic, "Yesu." It is

[1] Arviragus, the son of the famous Cunobeline (the "Cymbeline" of Shakespeare), whose gold coins, minted at Colchester, are the gems of every collection, was resident at the time in the royal city of Caerleon-on-Usk, only
30 miles on the opposite shores of the Severn Sea, and was thus in a position to
satisfy himself as to the peaceful intentions of the Christian missionaries.
Caerleon became one of the chief centres of Christianity in Britain, and its
famous college of Druid philosophers was converted to Christian use. When
300 years later, the Diocletian persecution broke out, 10,000 Christians, with
their leader priests, Julian and Aaron, were martyred for the faith.

singular that the ancient Briton has never changed the name of the God he and his forefathers worshipped, nor has ever worshipped but one God.

The universe is in substance eternal and imperishable, but subject to successive cycles of dissolution and innovation.

The Soul is a particle of the Deity possessing in embryo all its capability. Its action is defined and regulated by the nature of the physical organization it animates.

The soul which prefers evil to good retrogrades to a cycle of animal existence, the baseness of which is on a par with the turpitude of its human life. The process of brutalization commences at the moment when evil is voluntarily preferred to good. To whatever cycle the soul falls, the means of reattaining humanity are always open to it. Every soul, however frequent its relapses, will ultimately attain the proper end of its existence—reunion with God.

A finite being cannot support eternity as a sameness or monotony of existence. The eternity of the soul, until it merges in the Deity, is a succession of states of new sensations, the soul in each unfolding new capabilities of enjoyment.

In the following statement we have a remarkable fore-shadowing of Darwin's theory: "The creation of animals commenced with that of water molecules. Terrestrial animals are of a higher order than the aquatic, and rise through distinct gradations up to man. Animals approach the human cycle in proportion to their utility and gentleness; every animal may be killed by man in support or defence of his own life."

Cæsar, in his *Commentaries*, defines the Druidical doctrine of vicarious atonement with theological precision. "The Druids hold that by no other way than the ransoming of man's life by the life of man is reconciliation with the Divine Justice of the immortal gods possible."

The Druids believed in the existence of one Supreme Being of Whom they reasoned that He could not be material and that what was not matter must be God.

The Druidical teaching concerning Man's spiritual Nature is comprised in the following Triad:—

"In every person there is a soul,
In every soul there is intelligence:
In every intelligence there is thought,
In every thought there is either good or evil:
In every evil there is death:
In every good there is life,
In every life there is God."

"The Three primary principles of wisdom: Wisdom to the Laws of God: concern for the welfare of Mankind: and suffering with fortitude all the accidents of life.

"There are three ways of searching the heart of Man: in the thing he is not aware of, in the manner he is not aware of, and at the time he is not aware of.

"There are three Men that all ought to look upon with affection: he that with affection looks at the face of the earth; that is delighted with rational works of art; and that looks lovingly on little infants."

Other Druidic doctrines taught that—

"in creation there is no evil which is not a greater good than an evil. The things called rewards or punishments are so secured by eternal ordinances that they are not consequences but properties of our acts and habits. Except for crimes against society, the measure of punishment should be that which nature itself deals to the delinquent. Perfect penitence is entitled to pardon. That penitence is perfect, which makes the utmost compensation in its power for wrong inflicted, and willingly submits to the penalty prescribed. The atonement of penitents, who voluntarily submit themselves to death in expiation of guilt incurred, is perfect. The souls of all such pass on to the higher cycles of existence."

"The justice of God cannot be satisfied except by the sacrifice of life in lieu of life."

"Matter is the creation of God. Without God it cannot exist. Nature is the action of God through the medium of matter."

"The universe is matter as ordered and systematized by the intelligence of God. It was created by God's pronouncing His own name—at the sound of which light and the heavens sprang into existence. The name of God is itself a creative power. What in itself that name is, is known to God only. All music or natural melody is a faint and broken echo of the creative name."

One of the most sublime passages in the theological Triads

of Wales is that in which the Almighty is described on His return to Heaven after the great work of the creation:—

"Followed with acclamation, and the sound
Symphonious of ten thousand harps, that tun'd
Angelic harmonies."

Another "utterance" shows the spiritual character of Druidical teaching:—

"Let God be praised in the beginning and the end,
Who supplicates Him, He will neither despise nor refuse.
God above us, God before us, God possessing (all things),
May the Father of Heaven grant us a portion of mercy!"

The Welsh Triads, from their metre, says Matthew Arnold, are of undoubted antiquity and of special interest, as they show that the Druids were acquainted with the doctrine of the Trinity:—

"There are Three Primeval Unities, and more than one of each cannot exist; One God; One Truth; and One Point of Liberty, where all opposites preponderate.

"Three things proceed from the Three Primeval Unities; All of Life, All that is Good, and All Power.

"God consists necessarily of Three things the Greatest of Life; the Greatest of Knowledge; and the Greatest of Power, and of what is the Greatest there can be no more than one of anything."

The moral philosophy of the Order was upon an equally high plane—philosophy which became from constant repetition the creed of the people:—

"The three primary ornaments of wisdom: love, truth and courage."

"In three things will be seen the primary qualities of the soul of man: in what he may fear; what he would conceal; and what he would show."

"Three things that make a man equal to an angel: the love of every good; the love of exercising charity; and the love of pleasing God."

The Institutional Triads were as follows:—

The Three Primary Privileges of the Bards of the Island of

Britain are: Maintenance wherever they go; that no naked weapon be borne in their presence; and their testimony preferred to all others.

The Three Ultimate Intentions of Bardism: to reform morals and customs; to secure Peace; and to celebrate the praise of all that is good and excellent.

Three Things are forbidden to the Bard: Immorality; to satirize; and to bear arms.

The Three Joys of the Bards of Britain: the Increase of Knowledge; the Reformation of Manners; and the Triumphs of Peace over the Lawless and Depredators.

Bard

Stonehenge 'restored'

'*History cannot tell us [who erected the standing stones], for its records do not reach beyond the dawn of our civilization. But before that dawn there was the twilight of another civilization. History may ignore it; folk-lore may move in circles; nevertheless the vestiges remain. Great stones on the uplands and green ways winding across the chalk bear witness to the works of an ancient people long since fallen on sleep.*'

Dion Fortune in *Avalon of the Heart*

CHAPTER II

COMPARATIVE ANTIQUITY IN WILTSHIRE AND ELSEWHERE

"We can read Beth-el in a pile of stones and seeing where God has been, trust in Him."

LOWELL'S *Cathedral.*

"These antiquities are so exceedingly old, that no books do touch them, and that there is no way to retrieve them, but by comparative antiquity."

J. AUBREY, Antiquarian of Wilts, 1620-1700.

AND now that we have learned from Keltic lore that the religion of this "Island of Green Hills" was the worship of the "Lord of Hosts," "the Creator of the great lights" of the sun and moon, and not the worship of the heavenly bodies themselves, a further digression will be necessary, if we are to form any idea of the functions of the four *Great Seats* and two circles in the civilization of pre-Christian London. The only clue we have to the use of these and similar prehistoric monuments is in the descriptive titles and references in the Triads, to comparative antiquity on the Wiltshire downs, the headquarters of Druidical government, the burial place also of the "mighty dead" of the Stone, Bronze and Iron Ages. Here, on an undulating tableland, likened by John Evelyn to a "sea of verdure," some 20 miles long by 10 wide, lying between Marlborough and Old Sarum, girt in on the east by the valley of the Avon, we find the prototype of all circles and mounds in Britain.

On the North Downs stand in majestic solitude the two world-famous monuments of unknown antiquity, the Circle of Abury or Avebury, and Silbury Hill, unrivalled for size and scientific construction. On the meridian line, 20 miles due south of Avebury and originally connected by a fosseway, portions of which may still be traced, is the Cor Gawr, or great circle of the Ambresbiri, the Holy Anointed Ones, better known to us by its Saxon name of Stonehenge, from the Anglo-Saxon, stan, *stone*, hengek *gallows*. This name was given to the circle by Hengist to commemorate his treacherous massacre of the British princes on Mount Ambrosius (Vespasian's Camp,) May 1, A.D. 461, when, in his desire to denationalize the *sancta sanctorum* of Britain, the Saxon warrior commanded the bodies of the slain princes to be hung from the thirty lintels of the corona of the circle. Local tradition has preserved the memory of this desecration of Stonehenge, in the name of "Gallows Hill," by which the *via sacra* (the mile of road leading from the Mount Ambrosius to the circle) is called to this day by the shepherds and country folk.

The derivation of the title "Ambres" or "Ambresbiri," the *Holy Anointed Ones*, is of special interest. We find the name occurring again in "Ambresbury Banks," a fine example of British earthworks, superbly situated on the highest point of Epping Forest, the site of a Druidical circle, of which only one or two stones remain. It was here that Boadicea, the British warrior-queen, is said to have made her last stand. A pillar in Sir Fowell Buxton's grounds near by records her defeat and tragic death.

The origin of the descriptive title Ambresbiri (the Holy Anointed Ones) may be traced to Holy Scripture, where the earliest instance of anointing stones is mentioned in Genesis xxviii., when young Jacob, on his journey to his unknown relations, sleeping one night with a stone for his pillow, had a celestial vision and a promise from God of the highest importance to him and to all mankind. He took the stone and set it up for a pillar and poured oil upon it and called the place Beth-el, the *House of God*. So famous was that patriarchal temple of Jacob that we find the Syrian Hercules, who built Tyre, represented with the Petræ Ambrosiæ on the coins struck by that city in honour of him as their founder. Tradition says that this stone, upon which Jacob's head rested, was conveyed to Egypt, thence to Ireland and from there to Scone near Perth. Edward I, on his conquest of Scotland, carried it to Westminster, where it has been ever since, under the Coronation Chair. Preaching at Westminster Abbey on September 17, 1911, Archdeacon Wilberforce said that it fell to his lot during the preparations at the Abbey for the Coronation to guide to the Stone a well-known antiquarian, who had made a special study of its history. "He was convinced," said the Archdeacon, "that it was the stone on which Jacob rested his head when he had the vision of angels at Bethel, and that from that night it was considered sacred and carried from place to place. He believed it was this stone that Moses struck and that it was carried by the Israelites during their forty years of wandering. He showed me a big cleft in the back from which he believed the water gushed out. He showed me, also, two much-rusted iron staples deeply sunk, one at each end, which I had never noticed before, on which it was carried." The prophecy that, wherever the stone rested, Scottish blood should reign, had been literally fulfilled.

The great solar clock of the Ambresbiri, the "Measurer and Regulator" of time, the Greenwich Observatory of the Ancients, Stonehenge, differs from all other British circles in construction, and, as it is unique and throws no light on the circles of the Metropolis, need not be described. Suffice it to say that Sir Norman Lockyer has been able, from the sun itself, to fix the date of the "Wonder of Wilts" as 1680 B.C. with a possible error of 200 years either way, about the time of the death of the Patriarch Jacob and his burial in the land of Canaan.

There is one point, however, that may be mentioned in connexion witñ the Ambresbiri. A large portion of down half a mile from Stonehenge is still called the "Fair-field," and near it is the Cursus, or race course. This was doubtless the camping-ground for the pilgrims who attended the great solstitial festivals in their thousands. The Cursus, like the Circle itself, has been proved from scientific measurements to have had an astronomical significance, to which Mr. Griffith refers in his notes. The traditions of the old festivities and pastimes on the Wiltshire downs survive to this day in May-day or Garland-day holiday, the May Queen, the Maypole dance, Jack-in-the-Green, and in the part of London called Mayfair, where in the Middle Ages great fairs were held. Whit-Monday, Club-feast, Bean-feast, Midsummer Holidays, Harvest Homes, Harvest Suppers, dancing and feasting at the time of the Harvest Moon, and the Wassail Bowl of mead and metheglin (made from honey and honeycomb), are one and all echoes of the ancient British holidays.

The circles of Abury and Stonehenge and the vast earth-mound of Silbury Hill have been called the "British Pyramids," from their astronomical construction, and because, like the Pyramids of Egypt, thcy are surrounded by the tombs of kings. From Stonehenge 200 tumuli may be counted, among them the "seven old kings" and the "seven new kings" barrows (barrow = a Hebrew word signifying a heaped-up *pit of lamentation*). Barrows of the Bronze Age cluster more thickly round Abury, says Dr. Thurnam. Sir R. Colt Hoare spent fifteen years and a private fortuue in the thirties of the last century in opening 485 of these burial-mounds and in recording their contents; many objects taken from these prehistoric graves may now be seen in the British Antiquities Department of the British Museum. The tombs in this vast cemetery (Heb. a sleeping-place) have been made with the greatest reverence for the dead, not of the chalk of the district, but of earth brought from a distance. From far remote ages cremated, doubled up, or lying full length facing the sun at its noontide glory the mortal remains of succeeding generations of British princes, priests and leaders were here interred, decked in gala array of amber or jet necklace, bronze and gold ornaments, with their finely polished stone, bronze and iron weapons beside them, fully equipped for their future life in the great hereafter. Jet and amber were esteemed by the Ancients as more precious than gold, on account of their electrical properties. An amber necklace of 1,000 beads is mentioned in one of the Triads. Ezekiel, prophetically exulting over the fallen armies of the Egyptians, Persians, and other nations, refers to the custom of burying the leaders with their weapons of war beside them. "They shall not lie with the uncircumcised, which are gone down into hell with their weapons of war, and they have laid their swords under their heads" (Ezek. xxxii. 27).

In these days, when the British-Israel question is so much to the fore, it is of interest to note the striking resemblance traceable between the prehistoric British cemetery on the

Wiltshire downs and that of the Israelite leaders in Palestine. The embalmed remains of Joseph were brought to Gerizim, the "Mount of God," the ashes of Eleazar, Phinehas, Joshua, Barak, Jael, Heber, Jeroboam, Omri, Ahab, Jehu, Jehoahaz and Joash all lie around the sanctuaries of Beth-el and Gerizim in Samaria, 20 miles apart, as are the sanctuaries of Abury and Stonehenge in Wilts.

Cæsar tells us that belief in the immortality of the soul was the groundwork of British faith: it took from them the fear of death and inspired them with motives of courage. May we not see in this Westminster Abbey of pre-Christian times a foreshadowing of the tombs of princes, priests and statesmen, warriors, poets and musicians gathered together in the Abbey at the present day, "a combination of things sacred and things common, a union of the regal, legal, lay element of the nation, with its religious, clerical ecclesiastical tendency, such as can be found nowhere else in Christendom?" (Stanley).

The Metropolitan Temple of Britain, Abiri, Aburi or Avebury (in Hebrew signifying the "Potentes," the "Mighty Ones," the Sun and Moon, the Canterbury Cathedral of Kymric times, is within a five-mile drive of Marlborough. In strictness, none of the Druidic circles can be termed *temples*, for the Druids taught there were but two inhabitations of the Deity—the Soul, the invisible, the Universe the visible Temple.

Of this magnificent structure only the vast earth-circle, a mile in circumference, 44 feet high and calculated to accommodate 44,000 worshippers, remains intact. The circles of the sun and moon, with their respective index stones, constructed of unhewn sarsens (a Phœnician word for rock), some weighing 70 or 80 tons, were wantonly destroyed at the beginning of the eighteenth century. Ten only of the 100 stones of the outer circle remain in their original position. Stukeley described how he witnessed ninety of the great monoliths brought low by the simple process of digging a trench about them; this was packed with straw, and then fired; the flames flaring up the sides, the stone soon became red-hot when the trench was filled with water and water dashed against the sides, speedily causing it to fall, cracked into pieces; these

This is possibly how Abury looked some 5,000 years ago when it was first erected as a Sun temple. The surrounding ditch may have been filled with water, not as a barricade but to symbolize the site as a holy island.

'Thus, this stupendous fabric, which for some thousands of years has braved the continual assaults of the weather, and by the nature of it, when left to itself, like the pyramids of Egypt, would have lasted as long as the globe, has fallen a sacrifice to the wretched ignorance and avarice of a little village, unluckily placed within it.'

William Stukeley

were then taken to build the cottages and pig-sties that now occupy the site of one of the finest pre-historic monuments in the world.

There is no other circle in Britain that can compare to Abury either in size or construction. A journey to Darab in Persia would be necessary in order to find a prehistoric monument of similar dimensions and design. Sir William Ouseley, Plenipotentiary to the Court of Teheran in the twenties of the last century, figures and describes a vast circle he came across in his journey through this little-known country, which he likens to Abury. In these days of travel and research would that a thorough investigation of this solitary Persian circle could be made and its scientific construction compared with the desecrated and ruined remains on the Wiltshire downs.

The circles of the "Abiri" (the Mighty Ones) were approached from East and West by an avenue of upright stones, each a mile long, in the form of a serpent, symbolic of the sun's path through the zodiac. The head of this serpent, represented by an oval structure to this day called the "Sanctuary" by the country folk, consisted of concentric lines of upright stones. This head rests upon an eminence known as Overton or Hakpen Hill, which commands a view of the entire structure, winding back for more than two miles to the point of the tail, towards Beckhampton. Hakpen in the old British dialect signified Hak, *serpent*, Pen, *head*, i.e., head of the serpent.

In our own cathedrals we have the sign of the zodiac, represented as sacred emblems on the tiles of the sanctuary floor at Canterbury and Rochester, and the agricultural labours of the year frescoed on the chancel-roof of Salisbury Cathedral; at Waltham Abbey the signs of the zodiac and the labours of the twelve months were represented upon the flat beams of the Norman roof; these were repainted, when the Abbey was restored (1859-60), by Sir E. Poynter, President of the Royal Academy. In the vestry of this magnificent Abbey we find the following Scripture references showing that the signs of the zodiac are not necessarily connected with pagan worship. From the same source also we learn that, according to Josephus, the signs of the zodiac were engraved together with the names of the twelve tribes on the breast-plate of the high priest. If the Druidical religion had been sun-worship we may be perfectly certain these signs of the sun's path through the heavens would have been ignored.

A curious serpent-shaped mound near Oban, about 300 feet in length, curved like a huge letter **S**, wonderfully perfect in anatomical outline, is described by Miss Gordon Cumming in her book on the Hebrides: "The whole length of the serpent's back is constructed of symmetrically placed stones, set like the vertebrae of a serpent. In the Eildon and Arran district, wherever Druidic remains were found, there were mounds of serpent form."

On the side of Hakpen Hill was discovered a few years since, in ploughing, the cremated remains of the body (probably of a Druid priest) interred with two fine bronze armlets. These are now in Mr. J. Brooke's museum at Marlborough.

Immediately south of the circle and its adjunct Silbury Hill, ran the grand old fosseway of the Wansdyke (*gwahan*, separated), the division dyke, the boundary of the Belgic kingdom, which led east and west across the downs. This ancient road is said to have been drawn by the King Divitiacus, mentioned by Cæsar in his *Commentaries*. He built the neighbouring town of Devizes, so called from his name, and most probably the city of his residence. Trackways and fosseways intersected the dry chalk downs in all directions. These all converged on the Wansdyke, and where the land has not been thrown into cultivation may still be traced. Along these ways we may picture bands of pilgrims winding in procession as they journeyed from remotest districts to the place of National Assembly, the "Primary Earth Circle of Britain," where the assizes were held simultaneously with the great solstitial festivals. It is to these General Assemblies at "*Abiri*," Abury or Avebury, that the fundamental principles of the unwritten English constitution have been traced—that unique combination of Church and State Government that has come down along the ages; in the consistory courts held in some of our oldest cathedrals to this day, and in the word court, from the Keltic cor, a circle—courts of justice, circuit of the judges, derived from the ancient practice of administering justice within the precincts of these uncovered judgment seats between the hours of sunrise and sunset. Perhaps the words of Homer may be taken as describing the proceedings within the circle of "Abiri": "And Heralds kept order among the folk, while the Elders on polished stones were sitting in the sacred Circle and holding in their hands staves . . . there before the people they rose up and gave judgment each in turn" (I. l., xxiii).

Keltic tradition affirms that it was within the circles of Abury that the institution of the Gorsedd had its origin, a national institution not known out of Britain. The term is applied both to mounds and circles, as also to the Assemblies, in the same way as we now use the word "parliament." What relation precisely Aedd Mawr's Order, and its "Places of Assembly" held to the Civil Government it is, however, impossible to tell at this distance of time; that Druidism had retained in a great degree its original purity is practically certain for several reasons: the inaccessibility of the island, its freedom from invasion and the character for sanctity and integrity of the Kymry, its first colonizers. Probably at first the Gorsedd Assemblies were of a purely spiritual and temporal character; but that in course of time a political element crept in appears likely, as Edward I, for political reasons, forbade the holding of Eisteddfods—the Session of the Gorsedd. In the national Gorsedds and Eisteddfods of Wales the traditions of the Druidic Assemblies on the Wiltshire downs survive to this day.

Silbury, or the *Marvellous Hill*, the Mother of the Llan-din, or Parliament Hill, and of all our British sacred mounds, is finely situated a mile south of the circle of Abury, midway between the two extremities of the serpentine avenues leading up to the circles. Silbury covers 5 acres of ground, and is said to be the largest artificial mound in existence. Its less familiar Keltic title of Cludair Cyvrangon, literally translated the "piled" or "heaped mound of cognitions," Cotsworth's scientific investigations have proved to be an absolutely true definition of this remarkable earthwork. In his *Rational Almanack*[1] he throws light on the terraced lines, so frequently to be seen alike on natural and artificial "high-

[1] See Cotsworth's *National Almanack*, p. 305, published in York, 1900.

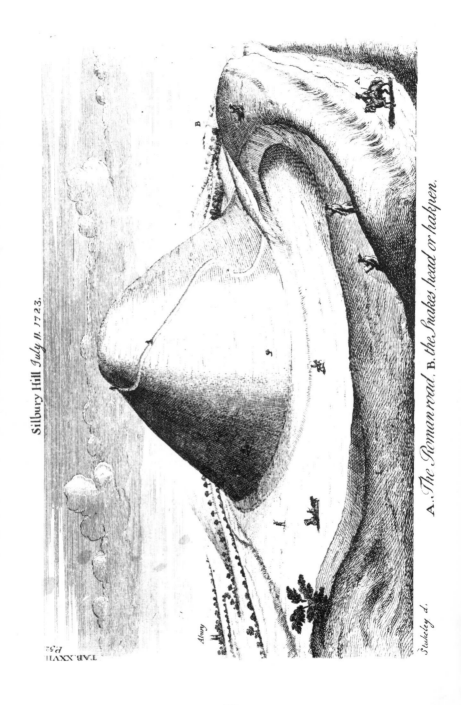

A..The Roman road. B. the Snakes head or harkpen.

Stukeley d.

Alwy

places," lines which are often taken for sheep runs, but which practical experiments have now proved were drawn with consummate skill by the astronomer priests to enable them to fix the four religious festivals of the year and the calendar.

> "The 30° slope of Sylbury not only enabled the Druid astronomers to sight the visible daily elevation between the equinoxes and the winter solstice, but also as the midday sun rose from the spring equinoctial footing to its mid-summer solstice height, it would be graded up the slopes to its turning point on the top north edge and down again to the autumnal equinox as autumn approached. In that way the four seasons of the year could be clearly indicated and comparative records kept by notching the daily and monthly points upon logs laid up the north meridian slope, as was done by the old clog almanacks which were used over Northern Europe ages before printed almanacks were invented."

We are bound to say there is a difference of opinion on this point, and that Rice Holmes and others refuse to accept the astronomical explanation of British mounds and circles. These objections are ill-founded, we consider, as they leave out a great deal of accumulative evidence which must have weight.

Silbury Hill is artificial, except where a natural hillock was partly utilized, and surrounded, as all these British sacred mounds were, with a deep trench. The great earthworks of a modern railway are the result of labour assisted by science and capital, and made with a view to profit; but Silbury Hill, symbolizing the whole earth surrounded by the ocean, and other mounds and high places of the same kind, were raised in remote antiquity by men whose ardent piety prompted them to make these herculean efforts to "draw nigh to God." Dean Stanley tells us "the ancient Phoenician and Canaanite religion may be called a religion of the 'hilltops.' " and so surely may be the primitive religion of Britain. For nowhere else in the western world are sacred mounds found in such abundance. [1] The "Mound of the Congregation" referred to

---

[1] Amongst the Gorsedds' or "high places," personally known to the writer, are: Arundel (Sussex); Bailey Hill (York); Brent Knoll; Mount Bures (Essex); Canterbury Dane John; Cadbury Mound; Caerleon; Cardiff; Chichester;

in Isaiah xiv. 9 is said by a Welsh writer to have been of the same type as our British "Places of Assembly," but whether any of the "high places," or "mounts," mentioned in Holy Scripture were artificial mounds we have been unable to ascertain. Nevertheless the Sinai of the new Law, the Sermon on the Mount, has for ever sanctified their use, in the declaration, this time final, of the Divine Will.

In the Triads, Silbury is referred to as one of the three mighty achievements of the Isle of Britain:

"The raisng of the stone of Ceti,
The building of the work of Emrys,
The heaping of the pile of Cyvrangon."

The stone of Ceti is the great cromlech on Cefn Bryn, Gower. The "work of Emrys" is an allusion to the Ambres or Embres of Stonehenge. Sir John Rhys tells us that the name Ambres or Ambrosius became Emrys in Welsh. The pile of Cyvrangon is, as we have stated, Silbury Hill.

In another Triad we find a very clear definition of the political system practised by the Druids within the Metropolitan Circle of Abury, which may be regarded as the origin of many of our institutions at the present day. The three pillars of the Commonwealth of the Isle of Britain:

"The Jury of a Country,
The Kingly office,
The Function of a Judge."

The "King's Bench" in the great Judgment Halls of Winchester and Westminster, to which the kings of England were formerly "lifted" before proceeding to their coronation, is said to trace back to the ancient practice at Abury of placing the King on a stone sedd or seat within the precincts of the "Supreme Seat," or "High Court," after that, by the "Voice

Cambridge; Exeter; Eton Montem; Harkness; Herefordshire Beacon; Marlborough; Malvern; Montacute; Maes Knoll; Maiden Castle (Dorchester); Norwich; Oxford; Rochester; Silbury; Sinodun; Old Sarum; Sol's Hill (Bath); St. Michael's Mount (Din Sol), Wallingford; Windsor; Whitfield's Mound (Blackheath, S.E.); also many others throughout the length and breadth of the land. It is curious to note that the translation of the Keltic name "Malvern" is literally *High Court*, or *Seat of Justice*. "Arthur's Round Table," Loughor, commands the Barry river.

of the People," he had been "elected." The Coronation Chair at Westminster and the Patriarchal Chair at Canterbury, constructed of three pieces of Purbeck marble, on which the Archbishops of Canterbury are enthroned, are relics of this prehistoric custom. The chairs of learning which the most capable are elected to fill are said to refer to the Gorsedd system of promotion by merit and not by favour. The procedure in the House of Commons has been traced to the same source, viz.: the office of "Black Rod," and the opening of the daily session with prayer.

The traditions of the "Great Assizes" of Silbury, held in the presence of a national assembly, presided over by the monarch, the arch-Druid, wisemen and councillors, survives in the fact that in three of our great cities a Gorsedd mound may be seen within the castle precincts. The Bailey Hill, York, is a notable example. At Oxford the first historic object that greets the eye, as we enter the town from the railway station, is the Great Seat of Justice of Kymric times, standing in close proximity to the modern Assize Courts. In a chamber in the interior of this prehistoric mound, the County Sessions, we were informed by the Governor, were formerly held. The conical mound of "Rougemont," Exeter, though now standing in private grounds, is within a few yards of the Law Courts. In the conquest of the West of England Athelstan seized the castle and carried on the continuity of the Gorsedd traditions by making the British Place of Assembly the seat of his executive. [1]

Cæsar tells us that the commanding mound on which the Cathedral of Chartres stands was used by the Carnutes for their great Assizes. At the base of this mound is a chapel in the solid rock, known as the "Grotte des Druides." May not the Consistory Courts, held within the precincts of many of our old cathedrals—notably the High Court of Durham, held in the Galilee—and the stone bench or Seat of Justice in the chancel of Southwark Cathedral, be the echo of the rude

[1] Henry III, 1267, held a Parliament under the shadow of the Gorsedd Mound at Marlborough, where the "Statutes of Marlborough" were enacted for restoring good government, after the Barons' Wars—another instance of the continuity of the Gorsedd traditions.

administration of justice by our forefathers, in their open-air courts, on the summit of these sacred mounds?

A still closer link with Kymric customs survives in the Court-leets, or Parliaments, held from time immemorial on the summits of the prehistoric mounds in the Keltic districts of Monmouthshire, Devon and Cornwall. On the circular summits of Ynys y Crug (the field of the mound), near Pontypridd, Court-leets were held down to 1856, when the mound was destroyed in making the Taff Vale Railway. Place-names in the vicinity indicate that formerly criminal law was here administered. In Devon and Cornwall, Court-leets for the redressing of grievances and transaction of business connected with the manor were called "parliaments" and were known as "stannary courts" (from the Latin *stannum*=tin). These representative assemblies of the tinners were summoned by the Warden under a writ from the Duke of Cornwall, one of the oldest hereditary titles of the Royal Family. There is documentary evidence to show that Plantagenet, Tudor and Stuart monarchs took an active and personal interest in the administration of these local parliaments.

On Crockerntorre (tor=a *sacred mound*), Dartmoor, "parliaments" were held until 1759. Perhaps Westman's Wood (a corruption of wiseman) in the neighbourhood, a relic of the primeval forest, recalls the memory of the wisemen, who took part in the council. At Lydford, in the same district, Court-leetes were held until quite recently, and "Lydford Law" is described as reversing the ordinary methods of justice: "a man was hung in the morning and tried in the afternoon."

Lady Shelley, in her Diary, 1818-1873, gives the following interesting account of Crockerntorre, which, from an antiquarian point, is of special value: "We visited the Crockerntorre, the headquarters of Druid superstition, which rises abruptly from the Wiseman's Wood, below the Hill of Bards. This wood is a curious survival of the ancient forest. A tree that had been cut down a few years ago showed 700 circles, which, under a microscope, were so close together that Archdeacon Youdle, who examined it, was of opinion that it must have been in existence during the expulsion of the Druids and the destruction of their pagan rites. As the Stannary Court was, during the last century, held within the Druid Circle above the wood, it is probable that this tree was flourishing during the period of the Roman occupation."

May not the origin of the title of "Parliament Hill," bestowed on the Llandin at some unknown period, be traced to similar representative assemblies of the citizens, merchants and seafaring population of the Port of Londin?

Old records show that Parliament Hill, like the Bryn Gwyn (the White Mount of the Tower) and the Tothill, Westminster, and many other Gorsedd, was a royal seat, a demesne of the Crown. Edgar the Peaceable in 978 made a grant of the Manor of Hampstead to his minister, Mangold, who, dying without heirs, it passed again to the Crown, and was bestowed by Edward the Confessor on his Church at Westminster.[1] Court-leetes, still held in connexion with the Manor, are of purely local interest. But the traditions of the National Assembly of British times flourish to this day, in the thousands, members of all classes and of all denominations, who assemble every Sunday to listen to addresses from lay and clerical speakers of every shade of religious and political opinion, on the self-same site where the Ancient Britons held their *"Gorseddau."*

Duke and others, who have given much time and attention to the subject, consider these vast prehistoric remains in Wiltshire to have been a "planetarium," or representation of the system of the heavens. From Aubrey's MS. notes, plans and drawings in the Bodleian, which, for lack of funds, he was unable to publish, it might yet be possible to unravel the mysterious design which he was the first to note and record. In his Memoir it is said that, coming suddenly upon the weird circle and serpent shaped avenues, when hunting one day, the young Squire was so much impressed that from that time he gave up sport and devoted the rest of his life to making surveys, counting the stones and marking their positions, to the neglect of his own private affairs. Seventy years later, Dr. Stukeley, of St. Thomas' Hospital, an eye witness of the

---

[1] William the Conqueror bestowed the Gorsedd Mound of Totnes upon his follower Judhael, whose Bretons are said to have won for him the Battle of Senlac.

destruction of the avenues and circles, tells us he found Aubrey's notes of the greatest service when he set about his exhaustive survey and report on Abury, Silbury and Stonehenge, a diagnosis on which the Doctor spent five summers. It seems almost a national duty to publish data of such a trustworthy character, throwing light upon the birthplace and cradle of our national existence.

If the circle of Stonehenge, from its peculiar construction, does not come within the scope of our inquiry, the Welsh traditions concerning the great national festival of the summer solstice, the White-sun-tide must not be passed over. There are grounds for thinking, as we shall see later on, that the same kind of scene may have been witnessed from the majestic summit of the Penton and other sanctuaries in the British Isles. The Druids, it is said, by means of a most powerful reflecting mirror of metal called "Dyrch Haul Kibddar," filled the circle with a blaze of glory from on high. This is mentioned in the Triads as the *speculum of the all-pervading glance*, or of the searcher of mystery; one of "the Three Secrets of the Isle of Britain." A foreshadowing, maybe, of that first great Pentecostal gathering on the Holy Hill of Zion—the *Mount of Stone* (as the name Zion means).

The scene within the circle on the morning of Midsummer-day, as the rays of the Live-giver shone direct upon the altar within the Holy of holies, the Sacred Ark, Navis, or boat-shaped symbol formed by the massive trilithons, has been graphically described by a Welsh writer.

"We behold the hundred Druids on their knees at 4 o'clock a.m., June 21, waiting for the rising sun to appear, and when he arrives, suddenly flashing his beams like a winged cherub into the most Holy of holies. . . . The flashes of June 21 symbolized the descent of the Awen, or Holy Wings, the Druidic name for the Holy Ghost, the Comforter. In the Kimmerian language of Druidism, he is called Awen Hafen, or the *Wings of June*. The arrival of the Awen was greeted with the words 'Holy, Holy, Holy' by the kneeling multitude on the downs outside, and the sound of praise was like the murmuring of the ocean."

Stonehenge is the one and only prehistoric sanctuary which

SUNRISE AT STONEHENGE

57

carries on the continuity of its traditions as a "Place of Assembly" to this day. The summer solstice, now as of old, is a magnetic attraction to hundreds of sightseers, who gather together from all parts of the world at eight minutes to 4 a.m. on the longest day, June 21, to watch the sun glide majestically on his upward path from behind the consecrated Pillar, Index, or Hele (Greek helios, *the sun*) stone. It is not until the whole orb, slightly flattened by the refraction of the air, has come into view, that the requirements are fulfilled, and then the coincidence is exact and the sun appears, as if balanced on the apex of the stone. It is, perhaps, possible to imagine the effect, but to an actual spectator the picture is most impressive, and the dark mass of the bowing stone, as seen through the frame formed by the uprights and centre lintel of the circle, adds brilliancy and completeness to the effect of a sight never to be forgotten.

Mount Ambrosius, or Vespasian's Camp, as the Gorsedd attached to the circle is now called, where dwelt the Guardians of the Ambresbiri (the Holy Anointed Ones), is of little less importance than Silbury Hill, and is of greatest interest, as the *traditions* of this Great Seat come within historical focus. Like Silbury Mount Ambrosius stands a mile from the circle, but, unlike the artificial "Cyvrangon," the mound is a natural eminence encircled on three sides by a natural symbolic trench formed by the river Avon. On the western slopes of Mount Ambrosius, commanding the circle, are still visible the sighting lines like those on Silbury drawn by the astronomer priests, whose duty it was to watch the warning star of sunrise and sunset and other solstitial hours. All traces of the College of Philosophy have disappeared, where lived the Archdruid and Druids, the learned expounders of astrological signs, the training centre of the Bards and Ovates of the Order. It is not improbable, however, that if the grounds were examined, traces of the Great Hall might be discovered, made famous by the usurper Vortigern's betrayal of his countrymen to Hengist within its walls. The chronicles refer to the sojourn of Aurelius on Mount Ambrosius after the defeat of the Saxons. It was at this time that, at the suggestion of the prophet Merlin, the King determined to bring the famous blue stones from Kildare, and erect them within the circle of Stonehenge as a memorial to the British princes slain by the treachery of Hengist, known to history as the massacre of the "long knives." A corbel in Amesbury Church is said to be the representation of the Roman British King Aurelius, who, from the part he took in causing this memorial to be erected, was given the title of Ambrosius. Spenser in the *Fairie Queene* refers to this "doleful monument" of the Blue Stones.

According to a local tradition, a college of Druidesses dwelt at the foot of the Mount Ambrosius. It is probable that, as at Chislehurst, the mound is honeycombed with caves cut in the chalk, where these Druidesses lived. This appears still more likely from the discovery of Mr. C. F. Cooksey of a series of prehistoric chambers cut in an insulated hill called "Le Platon" in the department of the Eure, France. It was the duty of the Druidesses to tend the sacred fire in the circle.

These Druidesses are referred to in one of the "songs" as "those defenceless ones" who were protected by Eidol or Emrys, the "Harmonious One," who escaped from Hengist's base massacre of the British chiefs. They are thought to be the same as the priestesses mentioned elsewhere as "Gwyllion."

In the Mabinogion we find the interesting tale of the defence of the circle by Eidol, the high-priest entrusted with the guardianship of the Ambresbiri, and it is related how the Arch-Druid overthrew the old religion, by riding armed into the centre of the circle, by this very act profaning the sanctuary, hitherto consecrated to the promotion of peace; and throwing his lance upon the Druidical altar, proclaiming the new religion—a religion adopted, as in no other country, without bloodshed or opposition of any kind. Missionaries are said to have come over from Glastonbury, only fifty miles away, soon after their arrival in the Isle of Britain, to instruct the guardians of the Ambresbiri in the Christian faith. That it was readily accepted we learn from a Welsh Triad, which mentions Amesbury as one of the "Three great cors of Britain, in which there were 2,400 saints; that is, there were 100 for every hour of the day and night in rotation, perpetuating the praise of God without intermission." Hence, as

Mr. Guest observes, "the Choir of Ambrosius was probably in the middle of the fifth century, *the* monastery of Britain, the centre from which flowed blessings of Christianity and civilization."

If we can find no record of the date of the foundation of a convent attached to the Abbey of Amesbury, we know from documentary evidence that from early Christian times in Britain, there was an establishment which appears to have been the favourite retreat of Royal ladies. Queen Guenever, when she fled the Court (in the first half of the sixth century), took shelter in the holy house of "Almesbury," and later on became Abbess. Queen Ælfrida, in atonement for the crime of murdering her stepson, Edward the Martyr, founded a Benedictine nunnery at Amesbury 980. Alfred the Great made his scribe Asser, Abbot of Amesbury. In fact, "Vespasian's Camp," remained Crown property, until Henry VIII bestowed it upon Edward, Earl of Hertford, afterwards Duke of Somerset.

It may interest some of our readers to know that the only visit that Royalty appears ever to have paid the "British Pyramids" was when Charles II was escorted to the top of Silbury in 1663 by Aubrey, who was investigating the antiquities at the time. He had the honour and gratification of taking the King and the Duke of York to the summit, or, as the Welsh would express it, the Pen y Byd (top of the world) and of there pointing out to his Majesty the marvellous "prospect," from this cyclopean monument, of the temples, earth circle, serpentine avenues, cromlechs and earthworks that lay around, and together with the countless tombs of the "mighty dead." A few years before, King Charles had spent a less agreeable hour at Stonehenge while waiting for the friends who were to assist his escape after the battle of Worcester, and had then employed himself by counting the stones over and over, in order to test the tradition that no one could count them twice alike, which he convinced himself was a vulgar error. It may have been the King's acquaintance with the astronomical circles of the Ancients in Wiltshire that suggested to him (a keen lover of science) the erection of an observatory in his own royal park at Greenwich—an observatory that occupies as unique a position in its way as Stonehenge of old, inasmuch as Greenwich at the present day is the first meridian of longitude, and practically gives time to the world.

Within the grounds of Greenwich Observatory is a well of unknown antiquity, an interesting link with prehistoric times. This well was used by Flamstead, the first Astronomer Royal, for making daylight observations; an old print preserved in the Observatory is now the only record of its existence, Sir George Airey having had it covered up. We shall have occasion to refer to the history of these ancient telescope wells later on, in connexion with others of the kind. There is little doubt but that Wren's building, from its commanding position, stands upon the site of an ancient British observatory mound. It is only within the last few years that the numerous barrows both in the park and on Blackheath have been levelled. As a "Place of Assembly" Keltic traditions cling still to the artificial mound on the Heath known as "Whitfield's Mound." Here the great preacher used to address 20,000 men at 5 a.m., and Lady Huntingdon (the foundress of so many Congregational chapels) and Lord Chesterfield (whose residence was near by) were among his eager listeners. The British custom and "right" of the people to use these prehistoric mounds as places of assembly survives to this day, and the mound is the one and only spot on the Heath where public speaking is allowed and meetings permitted.

The London group of "Holy Hills" has been so overshadowed by its subsequent commercial greatness that we must compare for their elucidation similar sites throughout the kingdom, which have been left undisturbed. Of these there are many, as the numerous place-names testify, that have either one of the little words *ton, tot, tor, twy, tyn*, signifying in Welsh a *sacred mound* and other forms depending on or in combination. In the towns and villages where such names occur, and in many another beside, is to be seen either a natural eminence, the contour of which shows signs of having been graded and terraced like the slopes of Silbury Hill and Mount Ambrosius, or there is an artificial conical Gorsedd

61

mound which has given its name to the place. Totnes, bound up with the fortunes of Brutus, the reputed founder of London, is a good example of this kind. Sometimes the artificial Gorsedd crowns the summit of a natural height as oh Old Sarum and Montacute, or as at Windsor, where the "Round-Table Mound" carries on the continuity of its historic traditions as a *Great Seat* or *Throne of the Monarch* to this day.

The Keltic termination *ton* occurring so frequently in the names of the suburbs of London suggests that even in Kymric times the population was sufficiently large in these districts to need a place of assembly. The traditions of Kennington Common point to a "ton" or a place of national assembly having been there at one time, for the ancient "right" of holding public meetings still survives. The Chartists availed themselves of this, when on April 10, 1848, they held their great mass-meeting on the rough piece of waste ground known as the Common. Whilst their leader O'Connor was addressing the malcontents, entreating them not to damage their cause by violence, an eagle, soaring over their heads in the direction of the Houses of Parliament, was hailed as an excellent omen. It was Frank Buckland's bird, which had escaped from his father's garden at the Deanery, Westminster, and was making its way home.

In the 'fifties, the Common was enclosed by the Prince Consort, and is now a public garden, for Kennington is a royal demesne, belonging to the Duchy of Cornwall. Probably it was at this time that the mound was levelled. The ancient privileges of the "ton" are preserved, however, on a triangular piece of ground fenced off for the purpose (the site probably of the mound), where a notice board states that here public meetings may be held. No better example could well be found of the truth of Disraeli's words, "a tradition can neither be made nor destroyed."

Another example of the survival of the traditions of these tons, or sacred mounds, is in Somerset, where until a few years ago the people of Welling*ton* were wont to assemble on the famous height that towers above their town, and there, in the dawn, drink to the health of "all their friends round the

Wrekin," just as they had done 3,000 years ago under the auspices of the Bards and Druids.

How large the sacred mounds, or Gorsedds, entered into the domestic as well as the religious lives of our forefathers, we learn from a custom of the Beltan, or spring festival, when the sacred fire was brought down by means of a burning lens from the sun. No hearth was held sacred until the fire on it had been lit from the Beltan. The Beltan became the Easter festival of Christianity. The summer Solstice, or White-sun-tide—our Whitsun—and the mid-winter festival, when the mistletoe was cut with the golden crescent from the sacred oak, became Christmas. The Druids regarded mistletoe as a symbol of Holy Love, which descended from the air as a heavenly gift. It was known to them by the name of Pren-awyr, the *air-plant.* From the many medicinal virtues attributed by the Druids to the mistletoe, it is called to this day in Wales "All Heal."

No city in the world probably ever presented a more majestic appearance than did the Kymric Porth of Llandin, or London, on the occasion of these great solstitial festivals, when the "Fires of God" blazed upon the summits of the four sacred mounds, the open-air sanctuary of our forefathers, roofed by the heavens, and floored by the bare earth. We may conjure up the scene, where the watery stretches reflected in molten gold the "pillars of fire," symbolizing the presence of God; we seem to behold the reverent forms of the white-clad Druids revolving in the mystic "Deasil" dance from East to West around the glowing pile, and so following the course of the sun, the image of the Deity. Simultaneously the voices of the Bards, singing in cadence, playing upon their glee-bearing harps with garlands upon their brows, shed abroad the praises of the Most High in the rhythmic measure of their national Triads. Dionysius tells us the Britons were crowned with garlands of ivy at their great festivals. Ivy, called Iorwg, implied the earliest creating attribute of Celi, or God; the Welsh still retain the word Celi, meaning the Deity or the Hidden One.

So little, however, is known of the pre-Roman history of London, and so scant are the traditions concerning the sacred mounds of the Metropolis, that rightly to estimate their importance as "places of assembly," or form any conception of their dignity as royal seats, it will be necessary to glance at the history of such well-known Gorsedds as Glastonbury, the Winton (St. Katherine's Hill, Winchester), the Windsor Round-Table Mound, and Eton Montem, mounds whose traditions are as closely identified with the activities of the Plantagenet, Lancastrian, Tudor and Stuart monarchs, as are those of the London Gorsedds with the personalities of the British kings.

To begin with Glastonbury, which succeeded the Druidical sanctuaries on the Wiltshire downs as the *sancta sanctorum* of Britain, and the burialplace of the late Keltic monarchs, as we learn from writers whose authority no one would venture to dispute. Next to Silbury Hill, Glastonbury Tor is the most majestic Gorsedd in the country. Rising to a height of 500 feet the "Holy Hill" is a landmark for miles round. Dean Alford, in his poem on "Joseph of Arimathea," pictures the saint and his twelve companions sailing up the waterway of the West, the Severn Sea, and as divinely guided to land on their mission when they should come within sight of a lofty green hill, "most like to Tabor's Holy Mount." Glastonbury Tor answering to this description the little company put in from the Channel and, making their way up the estuary of the Brue and the Parret (now dry land),[1] came upon a cluster of islands some twelve miles from the coast. The most imposing of these was the "Sacred Isle of Avalon," the "Mystic Isle," its base embowered in apple orchards. *Aval*, the Keltic for apple, the sacred fruit of the Druids, the emblem of fertility, thus gave its name of symbolic significance to the spot destined to become the Mecca of Christendom.

The Tor bears unmistakable evidence, from the terraced lines still visible on its contour, of its having been a Gorsedd, or "high place of worship," in prehistoric times. The peculiar aura of sanctity that enshrouds the traditions of one of the

---

[1] The Glastonbury monks banked up the river Brue 700 years ago; but there were large lakes to the N.N.W. of Glastonbury as late as the end of the seventeenth century. The last remains of a lake were drained away at the beginning of the last century. Parts of Glastonbury plain are below mean high watermark, and are flooded in wet weather.

GLASTONBURY TOR

oldest sanctuaries in Britain may be attributed to the probability that the Druid astronomers, the Wisemen of Britain, had made a simultaneous discovery with the Magi of Persia of the star of prophecy, whose appearance it was believed by the Eastern philosophers would inaugurate a new kingdom and a new dispensation. For so many centuries before the Christian era there had been constant communication between the chief port of Palestine and the trading stations of Britain, that it would have been most remarkable if the Druids, extolled by Greek and Roman writers alike as the great teachers of science of their day, should not have simultaneously, as it were, observed the long-expected "Day-Spring"—the star that should rise out of Judah.

About a mile from the "Sacred Isle of Avalon" was another small island known as Inis Vytren, or Glass Island, to which the Saxons gave the name of Glastonbury. Dr. Bulleid's recent discoveries and excavation of the pile-dwellings, which fringe its margin, have revealed to us the daily life of a highly civilized community some 300 years before the Roman conquest. Somerset is supposed to be derived from the tribe-name "Seo-mere-sactan"=dwellers by the Sea Lakes—the descriptive Keltic name probably of the numerous inhabitants of the Lake-dwellings. Professor Boyd Dawkins described the busy seafaring population of these islets as in—

"touch with the Mediterranean peoples as with those of Gaul. The industrial arts are well known, spinning, weaving, pottery-making, and work in glass, bronze and iron, as well as the most admirable carpentry. The inhabitants in their lighter moods gambled with dice that may have been derived from Italy, and amused themselves by cock-fighting with birds probably obtained from Gaul. We get this idea of the pre-Roman dwellers in Somerset in place of the woad-painted savages of our historians."

Dr. Arthur Evans tells us that the Romans carried off some of the Britons to Rome to teach them the art of enamelling. It is most satisfactory to find evidence of this statement in the actual material of glass-making unearthed in the Lake dwellings of Inis Vytren, literally "Glass Island." Fine specimens of richly enamelled horses' trappings may be seen in the British Museum, and the bronze shield found in the Thames near Battersea, adorned with bosses enclosing enamelled swastika designs, Rice Holmes describes as the "noblest creation of Late Keltic art."

That Inis Vytren, "our little Western Venice," as the Professor aptly calls this centre of prehistoric trade and civilization, was known by repute to St. Joseph of Arimathea, himself a rich merchant, there can be but little doubt from the fact that legendary traces survive to this day of the presence of Joseph and other Jews trading with the ancient tin-miners at Marazion; while in remote mining districts, where tin is blasted, the miner shouts "Joseph was in the tin trade," a bit of folklore that may have had its origin in the legend that "Joseph of Arimathea came in a boat to Cornwall and brought the Child Jesus with him, who taught him how to extract the tin and purge it out of the Wolfram." The ancient presence and influence of the Jew in Cornwall is marked and undeniable —names and places like "Bowejan" (abode of the Jews), "Trejewag" (Jews' village) and Market Jew Street, at Penzance, being well-known examples of such influence, and these, as well as the historical "Jewish windows" in St. Neot's Church and other Jewish monuments and memories, abundantly supplement the older traditions of "Jews' houses," "Jews' tin," "Jews' leavings." The very route of the tin-traders across Gaul described by Diodorus Siculus in the time of Augustus was the very same that was afterwards chosen by Joseph of Arimathea, whose footsteps from Marseilles to Morlais and from thence to Britain are traced in a most interesting way by Taylor in his *Coming of the Saints.*

The peaceful intentions of the Jewish missionaries being apparent, at the petition of Joseph and his friends, says William of Malmesbury, the historian of Glastonbury, the British King Arviragus gave them for their habitation twelve hides of land; a gift that is mentioned in Domesday. On this ground the very disciples of our Lord built of mud and wattle, thatched with reed after the manner of the country, the first Christian Church, not only in Britain, but in the world. With Greek rites, a Greek Easter, and a Greek ordination, here the disciples lived in separate huts and worshipped in the lowly sanctuary.

Arviragus is stated in the Chronicles to have been one of the later founders of Caerleon-on-Usk, the ancient seat of the Silurian princes, thirty-four miles only from Glastonbury on the opposite coast of the Bristol Channel. This ancient port of South Wales is described as rivalling Rome in its splendours of royal palaces and gilded roofs. Spenser pays his tribute to the British king in the lines:

> "Was never king more highly magnifyde
> Nor dread of Romans was than Arvirage."

It is further recorded that Arviragus was baptized by St. Joseph and adopted the Christian faith.

> "Joseph converted this King Arviragus
> By his prechying to know ye lawes divine
> And baptized him as write hath Nennius
> The chronicler in Brytain tongue full fyne
> And to Christes lawes made hym enclyne
> And gave him then a shield of silver white
> A crosse end long, and overthwart full perfete
> These armes were used throughout all Brytain
> For a common syne, each man to know his nacion
> And thus his armes by Joseph Creacion
> Full longafore Saint George was generate
> Were worshipt here of mykell elder date."

In the course of time Joseph of Arimathea and his companions died and were buried on the south side of the little chapel he had built of wattle. From this time the cemetery of Glastonbury took the place of the Wiltshire downs as the Westminster Abbey of British kings and saints. It was held in such awe and reverence that scarce any one dared to keep vigil there by night. No one built near it so as to obstruct the light. "Our fathers did not dare to use any idle discourse or to spit in it without some great necessity." Enemies and other naughty men were not suffered to be buried there, nor did any one dare to bring a horse, or dog, or hawk upon the ground; for if they did so it was noticed they "died forth-withe." So highly indeed was the privilege of burial in this sacred ground held, that people esteemed themselves happy in being allowed to increase the possession of the Church if only their bodies might rest under the Minster shadow. Many of the early British and Saxon kings and queens were buried at Glastonbury, King Coel or Hoel, the father of the Queen-Empress Helena, amongst them. But by far the most illustrious of the mighty dead was Britain's renowned warrior —King Arthur—whose tomb at Glastonbury, and Round Table at Winton, in a very interesting way link the "Gorsedds" of remote antiquity with all that is noblest and best in the chivalry of Christendom.

It is certainly very remarkable that neither the Romans, Saxons, or Danes ever made any attack upon Glastonbury and that this Church alone claims as her peculiar privilege never to have failed in her worship of the true Faith.

"There has been no break, no time when Christ has been set aside for any other name," says Professor Freeman. "Had Wells, or even Bath, laid claim to such an illustrious antiquity, their claims might have been laughed to scorn by the most ignorant. At Glastonbury such claims, if not easy to prove, were not easy to disprove. We read the tale of Phaganus and Dini-vianus, we read of Dractus and Gildas, and Patrick and David and Columb and Bridget, all dwellers in, or visitors to, the first spot where the Gospel had shone in Britain. No fiction, no dreamer could have dared to set down the names of so many worthies of the earlier races of the British Islands in the 'Liber Vitae' of Durham or of Peterborough. This is the one religious foundation which lived through the storm of English conquest and in which Britons and Englishmen have equal share. No-where is there the same unbroken continuity, at all events, of the religious life. At Canterbury Christ was worshipped by the Englishman, on the same spot as he had been worshipped by the Briton. But there was a time between, a time on which, on the same spot, or on some spot not far from it, Englishmen had bowed to Woden. But there was never a moment when men of any race bowed to Woden in the Isle of Avalon."

There is little doubt but that Glastonbury from this time

superseded the circle of Abury and Silbury Hill as the head-quarters of the national religion, now gradually becoming Christian under the patronage of the British monarchs, Arviragus and his successors. Winton (Winchester), some four centuries previously, it would appear, under Molmutius had become the supreme seat of civil government, and, as Dean Kitchen points out, is "the birthplace of our existence as a nation." The most striking feature of royal Winchester to-day, as of yore, is the Great Seat of the Winton (wyn, white or holy, ton=sacred mound), now called St. Katherine Hill, a circular chalk down standing boldly out in the valley of the Itchen. As on Silbury Hill and Glastonbury Tor, the graded slopes and encircling lines are still plainly visible, and stamp it at once as a prehistoric Gorsedd, the centre in purely Druidic times of civil and religious administration command-ing the old "White City" of Caer Gwent, [1] basking in a hollow of the downs. The earliest traditions of the Winton, like those of our London mounds, have come down along the ages embalmed in its descriptive Keltic name, which survives to this day as the official title and signature of the Mayor and the Municipality, and of the Bishop and the Diocese of Winton. Wykeham, also the founder of national education, with his consummate knowledge of the traditions of the Gorsedd, acquired in the reorganization of the British sixth century Order on the Windsor "Round Table" Mound, styles his college St. Mary de *Winton*, and not by the Romanized form of the name Winchester. We may look, therefore, on the majestic "Holy Hill" as the Psalmist of old looked upon his hills in Judea, as a sort of inspired testimony to the righteous government of God and the indestructibleness of His Church.

King Cnut made Winchester his capital, and working from Winchester, says Dean Kitchen, the historian of the old capital, aimed at uniting the two races on English soil and hoped so to consolidate his mighty lordship, which may almost be styled an imperial dominion stretching from the Isle of Britain to Scandinavia. The annals of the Cathedral

[1] The white or holy fortified enclosure, so called from the white walls of chalk with which Dunwal Molmutius enclosed the city.

record that Cnut gave to the old minster a property of three hides, called "Hilles." The Danish monarch thus followed the precedent set by his predecessor, the British King Arviragus, at Glastonbury, in presenting the "royal seat" as a gift to the Church. In this way the Winton passed into the hands of the Benedictines of St. Swithin's Priory. From them St. Katherine's Hill (as it came to be called from the dedication of a chapel[1] built on the summit) was purchased by Wykeham, who ordained, by statute, that twice daily his "seventy black-gowned scholars" should ascend the "Holy Hill" dedicated to their use as the recreation-ground of his college. Lord Selborne, in his Quincentenary Poem, thus alludes to one of the most cherished memories of Old Wykehamists:

"Four hundred years and fifty their rolling course have sped
Since the first serge-clad scholar to Wykeham's feet was led:
And stil lhis seventy faithful boys, in these presumptuous days,
Learn the old truths, speak the old words, tread in the ancient ways,
Still for their daily orisons resounds the matin chime:
Still linked in bands of brotherhood St. Catherine's steep they climb."

The Winton stands at about the same distance from the circle as does Silbury from Avebury. That Winchester Cathedral was erected on the site of a Druidic circle is practically certain from the fact that several Druidic stones were at one time to be seen in the Close. The late Dean Stephens pointed out one of these to the writer, near the King's Gate, a relic which he considered went far to confirm the tradition that Lleuver Mawr, "the Great Light" (known to Latin writers as Lucius), he, who in the Triads is described as "the first in the Isle of Britain who bestowed the privilege of country and nation and judgment and validity of oath upon those who should be of the faith of Christ"—the first Christian king (*circa* A.D. 170)—built the first minster on the site of a circle, and at the same time transferred the Druidic emolu-

---

[1] Cardinal Wolsey having transferred the endowment of St. Catherine's Chapel to his Oxford foundation at Christ Church, it fell into ruins, of which not a vestige remains.

ments to the maintenance of the Christian clergy. The old "Court House" in the Close the Dean regarded as another
link with Druidic times, recalling the days when the Arch-Druid held his courts of justice in "the face of the sun—the eye of Light," within the precincts of the open-air cor, court, or circle. Within the walls of this old timber-house, courts of justice were held, said the Dean, until the new Guildhall in the City was erected. In the Cathedral Close of Norwich is a similar Court House, with a notice over the little old doorway, "The High Court of Justice."

The earliest historical record of Winton (Winchester) as a "Gorsedd," i.e. a great seat of the monarch and a seat of government, is in 500 B.C., when, according to local tradition, Dunwal Molmutius made Winton his capital. In the chronicles of the ancient British kings it is stated "Dyfnwal ab Clodin, Duke of Cornwall, made all Britain one monarchy, which before was divided between five kings or dukes. . . ." Molmutius is said to have excelled all the kings of Britain in valour and gracefulness of person. After an interregnum of some years occupied by the contest of various claimants to the throne, as the representative by both paternal and maternal descent of the younger branch of the British dynasty, he was recognized Sovereign-Paramount by the Voice of the People, according to ancient British usage.

The citizens of Winchester have given Molmutius, as the founder of their ancient city, the foremost place of honour in a series of bas-reliefs on the façade of their new Town Hall, representing British, Saxon, Norman, and Plantagenet monarchs, whose names are interwoven with the traditions of "Royal Winchester." Of Molmutius' work as a law-giver and a road-maker we shall learn later on when we come to describe his connexion with the still older capital of London.

Having given precedence to the national Gorsedds of Glastonbury and Winton, we now turn to the royal Gorsedds of Windsor and Eton Montem, second only to them in interest.

The Windsor Gorsedd, the Win-de-Sieur, *the White or holy mound of the Sieur or Lord* (according to the Welsh derivation of the name), is the only Gorsedd which in unbroken historical continuity has literally fulfilled its Keltic title as *a great seat or throne of the monarch* from the sixth century to the present day. "Piled up," at some unknown period, on the summit of a natural chalk down—"a height that does at once invite a pleasure and a reverence from our sight" (Drayton)—"The Round-Table Mound," as it is usually called, crowned by Edward III's Round Tower, is the distinguishing feature of the "stateliest royal castle in Europe." In the Conqueror's time the majestic mound commanded vast woods of oak and beech, comparatively small portions of which still remain known as "Windsor Great Forest."

There is no doubt that this circular conical mound, 100 feet in diameter at its base, encircled by its symbolic trench, is entirely artificial. This has been proved by a shaft or well in the interior, which, when examined in 1885, was found to be lined with ancient masonry until it reached the chalk soil on which it had been erected. John Evelyn, who never allowed anything of a scientific nature to pass unrecorded in his diary, refers to "the well on the Mount," but makes no comment or remark about it.

One of the foremost scientific men of his time, a Fellow of the newly-founded Royal Society, in touch with the newly-appointed Astronomer Royal, it is probable that the old Squire of Deptford noticed this well on the Windsor mound from his knowledge of a similar shaft of unknown antiquity in the Greenwich observatory.

The Windsor Gorsedd enshrines for all time both Druidic and Christian ideals. The "Great Seat" owes its fame entirely to the magnetic personalities of two of our most illustrious and representative kings, "the noble Arthur, first of the three most Christian worthies of the world" (Caxton) and the romantic warrior-king, Edward of Windsor. Pre-eminent as national leaders, these monarchs were at pains to preserve the traditions of the British Gorsedd Assemblies in the respective institutions they founded for the promotion of chivalry. The British King Arthur, when he reorganized the Druidic Order on Christian lines, ordained that his "goodly Fellowship" of the Round Table should carry on the continuity of the

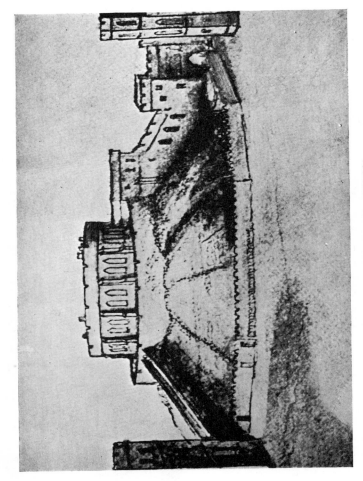

ROUND TABLE MOUND, WINDSOR
(From Ashmole)

Druidic custom, and celebrate national festivals on the summits of the sacred mounds, as their forefathers before them had done. Malory tells us of Round Table Assemblies held in London, Winchester, Camelot (Cadbury Mound), Caerleon; but the King's favourite "station" for the Whitsuntide festivities was the Windsor Table Mound. Froissart records show "Edward, King of England at this time, resolved to re-build the great castle of Windsor, formerly built and founded by King Arthur; and where first was set up and established the noble Round Table, from which so many valiant men have issued forth to perform feats of arms and prowess throughout the world." It is also from Froissart, the court chronicler of the time, that we learn it was a romantic pilgrimage Edward III and his young Queen Philippa made to Arthur's tomb at Glastonbury which determined the Plantagenet monarch to refound the British Order, revive the Round Table Assemblies, the tilts and tourneys of Arthurian days, and once again make Windsor the centre of European chivalry.

The first step taken was to instruct his young surveyor and secretary, William of Wykeham, to enclose the Gorsedd, the Round Table Mound of the British Kings' Assemblies, with a Round Tower. Within the walls of this unroofed enclosure the Knights of the Order of St. George and the Garter, from the day of the inauguration, St. George's Day, April 23, 1351, to the time of Charles II, celebrated the annual festival of the Order, which for antiquity and dignity take precedence of all others of the kind in Europe.

Edward III, following in the footsteps of the British king, the founder of the Round Table, whom he appears to have made his ideal, identified himself all through his reign with the interests of the national Church against the encroaching claims of the Roman see. Wykeham's inquiries into the traditions of the Order showed that the British Church of the first five centuries had been entirely free of papal control, and that one of the first acts of Arthur's reign had been to refuse the tribute demanded by special emissaries sent from Rome. It may have been this precedent set by his predecessor that determined King Edward to obtain a Bull from Pope Clement

VI (1348), declaring the Chapel of St. George a free chapel,[1] i.e. free (as had been the early British Church) of papal jurisdiction. The sovereign—the head of the order—and the Bishop of Winchester, the prelate, nominated the deans and canons, with appeal to the visitor, the Lord Chancellor. The royal chapel of St. George's, Windsor, may therefore claim to be the keystone of the Reformation, and as a religious foundation thoroughly organized in every detail of its constitution by fifty-four original statutes. St. George's College is the first in England founded "free" of the control of abbot or prior, and its statutes have been the model upon which all post-Reformation cathedral and collegiate staffs have been moulded. In his *Governor's Guide* the Duke of Argyll (Constable of the Castle at this time) reminds us that "Windsor takes precedence of Westminster, and that the succession of deans and canons of Windsor has not been interrupted for five and a half centuries. The Abbey was not refounded and made collegiate till 1603, under Queen Elizabeth." According to Moberley,[2] Edward III may be said to have begun the resistance to the Roman claims to supremacy which culminated in the rupture under Henry VIII, two hundred years later.

Another far-reaching benefit to the nation was the outcome of Edward III's revival of the British Order. His lowly-born secretary, William of Wykeham, upon when had devolved all the research and the organization of the College and the Order, had become so imbued with the importance of national education, in the spirit set forth in the national Triads and in the rules of the Round Table, that he resolved, when opportunity came, to found two colleges for the education of the "poor and needy," the one at Winchester, the other at Oxford. Promoted, by his royal patron, to the highest honours in the realm, after

---

[1] King Edward III obtained at the same time a Bull from Pope Clement VI, making his twin foundation of St. Stephen, Westminster, a free chapel and college. Dean and canons were appointed, much to the wrath of Abbot Littlington. It is probable that Wykeham designed the Chapel of St. Stephen's (destroyed by fire in 1836) and drew up the statutes of the College, but as the history of St. Stephen's has not been written, the only thing we know for certain is that Wykeham was one of the canons. The statutes of St. Stephen's College are said to be "lost," like those of St. George's College are said to be "lost," like those of St. George's College, Windsor, but probably, if search were made, they would be found.

[2] Moberley's *Life of William of Wykeham.*

twenty years' loyal and faithful service at Windsor, Wykeham succeeded to the see of Winchester, vacated by the death of his former patron, Bishop Edington, and in the same year was appointed Lord Chancellor.

One of Bishop Wykeham's first undertakings was to set about the foundation of his "Nurserie of St. Mary's, Winton," for "seventy poor scholars," who on the Druidical plan of promotion by merit and not by favour, were to pass on to his Oxford college, there to be trained in divinity and law as secular clergy. To give his young scholars experience in leadership, the "Father of Public Schools" ordained that the senior scholars should be entrusted with a certain amount of power and responsibility, and at the age of fifteen were sworn loyally to maintain the honour and corporate unity of their school and college. Thus the ancient laws of Chivalry were no longer confined to a few chosen leaders of noble birth, but they became the actual foundations on which the great fabric of national education had been reared. Among the very few of the Chancellor-Bishop's words that have been preserved to us, there is a simple saying often in his mouth which shows how deeply-graven in Wykeham's heart was the feeling which his motto, "Manners maketh man," expressed. "There can be no true dignity," he was wont to say, "where there is no high principle."

Strange, that in spite of Edward III's historical refoundation of the Arthurian Order on the Windsor Table Mound and the part played by Wykeham in its reconstruction, the authorities of to-day insist that King Arthur is a "mythical monarch," his "goodly-fellowship," the popular theme of European romance, "mere legend," and the Round Table in the Great Hall of Winchester Castle (for 400 years England's Old Parliament House) no genuine relic. The testimony of the earliest British historians, Gildas and Nennius, is ignored. The numerous references to Arthur's exploits, death and burial in MSS. (other than those of Geoffrey of Monmouth) in the British Museum, Bodleian and Cambridge libraries, we are told, are of no "historical value." Place-names and traditions go for nothing; and even the genealogies of the British kings, by virtue of which Henry VII claimed his title to the crown, are said to be "monkish inventions" and "utterly worthless" when we refer to these chronicles as proof of Arthur's personality. It was Henry Tudor's proud boast to be descended, not from Norman, or Plantagenet, but from the Keltic kings, Arthur and Cadwallader the Blessed, the last of his race to assume the royal title. The revival of the ancient Keltic-British element in the British monarchy, after centuries of eclipse, is a fact recorded in a striking way in Henry VII's Chapel, Westminster Abbey, where intertwined in the bronze closure round about the tomb of the founder of this magnificent mausoleum, may be seen the emblems of the House of Lancaster with those of the British King Cadwallader, the "Dragon of the great Pendragonship" of Wales. [1]

To dispute the antiquity of the Round Table is to attribute to our Crusader kings, Richard I and Edward I, a superstitious veneration for a relic, utterly beneath the dignity of two of our greatest national leaders, who, on the eve of their departure to the Holy Wars, assembled the Barons of England round its board, and delivered the kingdom into their charge. Moreover, if there had been any sort of doubt about the life story of the "First of the Knights"—the Founder of Chivalry—the Emperor Maximilian, "Der letzte Ritter," the "Last of the Knights," as he is called in Germany, would not have honoured the traditions of Arthur and his Round Table by a visit to Winchester Castle to see the relic on his return journey after his installation as a Knight of St. George at Windsor; nor would so great a lover of chivalry have caused a bronze statue to be made of Arthur and placed the first in order of the "Chivalry of Europe," whose effigies adorn his magnificent cenotaph at Innsbruck.

It is no compliment to Henry VIII either, to allow for a moment that this shrewd monarch would have taken his royal guest, Charles V, to spend a week at the royal castle, and on this occasion have had the Round Table taken down from the gable, overhauled and painted green and white, the liveries of the British order with himself depicted as sovereign, and in the centre the rose of York and Lancaster, or as some authorities say the rose of St. George. The names of the com-

[1] See Dean Stanley's *Memorials of Westminster Abbey.*

panions of the "Goodly Fellowship" inscribed on the margin by the Tudor monarch we have been able to identify with but one exception as owners of castles and demesnes in Monmouthshire, South Wales and Cornwall.

But the most convincing proof of Arthur's personality is the intangible hold on the imagination that the institution of the Round Table continues to exercise on the activities of the nation. In the Round Table Conferences we see noticed in the newspapers from time to time, when any important question affecting the higher interests of the nation arises, may be traced the survival and vitality of the spirit and principles of the Druidic and Christian Gorsedds held on the summits of the sacred mounds of Londinium, Winton, and elsewhere, in those centuries when the British constitution was in the making. Among the most notable "Round Tables" of our own own time may be mentioned the Round Table called by Bishop Creighton to discuss the ritual question; the Round Table summoned by the Archbishop of Canterbury to consider the Education Bill, and the Round Table held when the Veto Bill was the all-absorbing topic of national interest. Certainly the most historic Round Table was that summoned by Cecil Rhodes when Premier at the Cape. Indeed, Arthur's mantle would appear to have fallen on this great idealist and champion of chivalry, when he gathered the Matabele warriors around him, on that weird "place of assembly," the summit of the Matoppo Hills, and by an appeal to their sense of justice and chivalry, "all that makes a man," induced these armed warriors one by one to step forward and lay down his weapon at the feet of the "Great White Chief." And in this way a war ended which had harassed the country for years. In its beneficent and far-reaching results, Rhodes' achievement may compare not unfavourably with some of the many exploits of the "noble Arthur."

One other mound remains to be noticed before we return to the consideration of the London Gorsedds and the monarchs whose names are associated with the traditions of these prehistoric places of assembly. "Ea-ton" College, as the name is spelt in the letters patent of the An. Reg., 19 Henry VI, 1441, derives its title from the artificial mound known as Eton

Montem, or Sol's Hill, corrupted into Salt Hill. "Piled up" in remote antiquity on the watery meads that environ the royal college, the "ton," or *sacred mound*, formerly encircled by a stream, now partially diverted, was an ea, or island, hence the descriptive name of Ea-ton. It is only since 1840, when the triennial processions of the scholars to the Montem were discontinued, that the "Great Seat" has partly lost its original contour, from a slice having been cut off the base to widen the road. The great interest of the Eaton Gorsedd lies in the fact that Henry of Windsor (Holy Henry, as he was called by the people), in sympathy with the religious traditions of this ancient high place of worship, ordained by statute that the memory of the solstitial festivals should be perpetuated by the scholars on the self-same site where in pre-Christian times the praises of the Most High had been celebrated by the Druids.

In the College statutes elaborate directions are given for the due celebration of May-day. In the early morning the King's scholars were to go "a-maying" to the woods, bringing back the fragrant boughs with which they were to adorn the windows of the College, and a very human touch is given to this statute by the thoughtful young monarch's injunction, that if his scholars' feet were wet with the morning dew, they should change their shoes on their return. The autumnal Equinox in September was to be celebrated in much the same way by "a nutting" expedition to the woods, and to pick apples; the scholars were enjoined to give a portion of the spoils to their tutors. On both these occasions the whole school marched in procession, in a kind of military order, with music and flags, to the summit of the Montem.

But the great festival of the college the royal founder ordained should be celebrated about the time of the Whitesun-tide, on the Tuesday in Whitsun week, when, amidst every token of rejoicing, masters and scholars assembled on the summit of the Montem. For four centuries "Montem Day" was observed after this fashion. Money, or "salt," as it was called, was collected for the benefit of the captain of the school from the spectators. But after the railway was opened, about the middle of the last century, the crowds became unmanageable, the custom was discontinued and "Montem Day" changed to June 4.

In the grant of arms to his college Henry VI states his desire, not merely to equal, but to surpass his predecessors in munificence, and the wish that the work of his hands should be adorned with every possible splendour and dignity. It there expresses the truly royal sentiment that "if men are ennobled on account of ancient hereditary wealth, much more is he to be preferred, and to be styled truly noble, who is rich in the treasures of the sciences and wisdom; and is also found diligent in his duty towards God." As Wykeham's school of St. Mary Winton was the only public school then in existence, the royal founder went down to Winchester, where he remained a month, to study Wykeham's new system of education, and to copy the statutes, which the founder-Bishop had ordained should never be taken away from his college. It is recorded that the King frequently attended Divine Service in St. Mary's College Chapel, and, impressed with the beautiful proportions, the sacred numbers employed in the "days" of the large windows and the ground plan in the form of the ancient **T**-shaped cross, determined to reproduce Wykeham's plans in every detail, only on a more magnificent scale, for his own colleges at Eton and Cambridge.

It should here be remarked that Bishop Wykeham's love for Keltic traditions is shown in the design of his college chapels at Winton and Oxford, both built in the shape of a Tau cross. The great architect-Bishop's ground plan was followed by his two first scholars, Chicheley and Waynflete, in the chapels of their respective foundations at All Souls and Magdalen College, Oxford. This anticipatory cross, as it has been called, is that on which the brazen serpent was lifted up by Moses in the Wilderness, and was, according to tradition, the mark made upon the lintels at the first passover. It was a custom of the Kymry to place a cross of this form in the centre of the thatch of their circular dwelling.

Keltic survivals may be traced also in Waynflete's institution for the observance of May-day and the summer solstice; the former by the singing of the Latin hymn at sunrise on Magdalen Tower by the clergy and choir of his Oxford college, in which the townsfolk take part in the road below on "hoarse horns." Midsummer-day (the feast of the nativity of St. John the Baptist) the founder ordained should be celebrated by a sermon preached from the stone pulpit in the quadrangle, which was to be strewn with "fresh rushes" on this occasion. This was discontinued only in the nineteenth century.

In gathering up these scattered strands of historical evidence, we have endeavoured, however inadequately, to show that Kymric institutions in all the departments of polity, law, the executive and religion, underlie the spirit of the British Constitution.

ETON COLLEGE

CHAPTER III

FOOTPRINTS OF NOTABLE BRITISH MONARCHS

"A land of settled government,
  A land of just and old renown,
  Where Freedom slowly broadens down
From precedent to precedent.

*   *   *   *   *

"Where faction seldom gathers head
  But by degrees to fulness wrought
  The strength of some diffusive thought
Hath time and space to work and spread."

TENNYSON.

WITHIN the last half-century entirely new light has been thrown upon the prehistoric history of London and its mounds, by Schliemann's discoveries at Hissarlik, the ancient Troy in the north-west of Asia Minor. No longer need the story be regarded as fabulous, that Brutus the Trojan, the grandson of Æneas (the hero of Virgil's great epic), gave the name of Caer Troia, Troynovant or New Troy, to London. In site and surroundings, as we have already stated, there seems to have been considerable resemblance between the historic Troy on the Scamander and New Troy on the Thames. On the plains of Troy to-day may be seen numerous conical mounds rising from out the lagoons and swamps that environed the citadel hill of Hissarik, akin to those that dominated the marshes, round about the Caer and Porth of London, in prehistoric times. Sayce's researches, moreover, prove the Trojans and the Kymry to have been of the same stock. In his preface to Schliemann's *Ilios* the professor writes:

"Thanks to the discoveries in unearthing the remains of Ilium, we know *who* the Trojans originally were, that they belonged to the Aryan race, speaking a dialect that belonged to the Aryan family; so that we, as well as the Greeks, of the age of Agamemnon, can hail the subjects of Priam, King of Troy, as brethren in blood and speech."

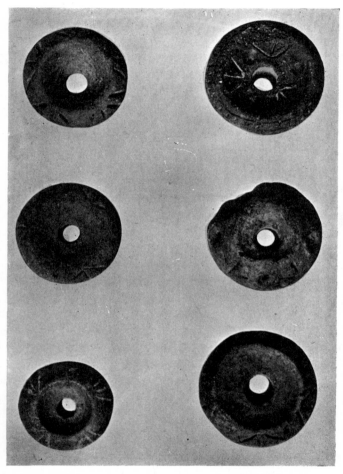

TERRA-COTTA WHORLS FROM HISSARLIK

Nor is material evidence lacking of a kinship between the Kymry of the Troad and the Kymric settlers in Britain in the religious symbols of their primitive worship. Schliemann discovered in the lowest diggings of Troy terra-cotta whorls incised with the hierogram of the Deity, the three rays or rods of light, a symbol of the "Awen," the "Holy Wings" or "Holy Spirit," from remote ages to the present day the badge of the Druidic Gorsedd. In the same diggings numerous other whorls have been found incised with the Svastika (in Sanskrit meaning an auspicious mark derived from Svasti "well" and as "to be"), a symbol of the sun, perhaps of the vernal sun, as opposed to the autumnal, therefore a natural symbol of light, life, health and wealth. These Hissarlik whorls lend additional interest to the beautiful enamelled svastika devices on the Late Keltic bronze shield in the British Museum, found in the Thames near Battersea, and point to Trojan and Eastern influence in this gem of British art and craft. A triangular variant of svastika appears upon several of the ancient Cornish crosses.

But, as modern authorities regard the story of Brutus, the reputed founder of London, as fabulous, before we examine the evidence that survives to the present day of the personality of the Trojan prince, it will help us to realize the possibility of the truth of the tradition, if we first glance at the account of the colonization of the isle of Britain, gathered principally from the Triads and Druidic remains collected by the eminent Welsh scholar and bard, Rev. R. W. Morgan (P. C. Tregynon).

In this ancient literature concerning the primitive migrations of the Kymry is one of the oldest recorded traditions of the Flood:

"Long before the Kymry came into Britain the Llyn Llion, or Great Deep (literally the abyss of waters), broke up and inundated the whole earth.

"The Island, afterwards known as Britain, shared the general catastrophe. One vessel floated over the waters, this was the ship of Nevydd Nav Neivion. In it were two individuals preserved—Dwy Van (the man of God) and Dwy Vach (the woman of God). By the posterity of these two the earth gradually repeopled.

"The ship of Nevydd Nav Neivion was built in Britain, and was one of its three mighty works.

"For a long time after the subsiding of the deluge the Kymry dwelt in the Summer Land, between the Sea of Afez and Deffrobani. The land being exposed to sea floods, they resolved, under the guidance of Hu Gadarn to seek again the White Island of the West, where their father, Dwy Van, had built the ship of Nevydd Nav Neivion.

"They journeyed westward towards the setting sun, being many in number and men of great heart and strength (*Cedeirn*, mighty ones, giants). They came in sight of the Alps, and then part of their migration diverged southward—these are the Kymry (Umbri) of Italy. The others, consisting of the three tribes of the Kymry, the Brython and the Lloegrys, crossed the Alps. Along either side of the Alps, near the sea, part of the Lloegrwys settled; these are the Ligurians of Italy and Gaul. Pursuing their course still further they crossed the River of Eddies, the Slow River, the Rough River, the Bright River (the Rhone, the Arar, the Garonne, the Loire), till they reached Gwasgwyn (Gascony, the Vine-land). Thence they turned northward and part of the Brython settled in a land they named *Llydaw ar y Mor Ucha* (the land or expansion on the Upper Sea Armorica). The Kymry still held onward until they saw the cliffs of the White Island. Then they built ships and in them passed over the Hazy Ocean (Mor Tawch) and took possession of the Island. And they found no living creature on it but bisons, elks, bears, beavers and water monsters. And they took possession of it not by war, nor by conquest, nor by oppression, but by right of man over nature. And they sent to the Brythons in Llydaw, and to the Lloegrysw on the Continent, and to as many as came they gave the East and the North of the Island. And the Kymry dwelt in the West. These three Tribes were of one race, origin and speech. These are the three Pacific Tribes of the Isle of Britain, because they came in mutual good-will, peace, and love; and over them reigned Hu the Mighty, the one rightful Sovereign of the Island. And they called the Island the White Island (Ynys Wen), and the Island of the mighty ones. Its name Britain, or Prydain, was not yet known."

This account is a very striking one. The date precedes, by many centuries, the earliest traditions of Greece and Rome. Its statements are in entire accordance with the results of the most recent investigations into the origin of languages and nations.

All the most ancient writers of Greece and Rome concur in stating that the Kymry or Gomeridœ, were under appellations slightly varied, the Primo-genital or oldest family in the world. Along their first habitation the shores of the Euxine and the Sea of Azov, they were known as Kimry or Kimmeroi; the peninsula which formed part of their dominions retains their name Kimria, corrupted into Crimea. South of the Caucasian Range they were called Gomrai.

Many of the most important positions in Armenia and around the Caucasus retain their primitive Kymric names. Gumre (the chief fortress and headquarters of the Russian forces), Van (the peak), Erivan (on the peak which Erivan is), Kars (the stone fort), Trezibond, Trasseguntum (the lower town), etc. A trivial detail, but one which shows kinship with the Kymry of the Caucasus, is the tradition that the art of making Cornish cream is practised only here and in Cornwall.

So also the great natural features of Europe retain the names assigned by the Kymry when they first penetrated its uninhabited forests and silent plains. Alp in Kymric is the rocky mount; Apennines, "the heads"; Cevennes, the backs or ridges; Pyrenees, the spires; Dòn, the nave; Tagus, the stream; Loire, the bright river; Pwyl, or Hwyl, the marsh; Rhen, or Rhine, the flooding river.

At Trèves (Trier), the capital of Belgic Gaul, which comprised not only Gaul proper so called, but the whole of Spain and Britain, most interesting material evidence of one of the earliest migrations of the Kymry is to be found. On the walls of the Rothes House, formerly the Rath-haus, a Latin inscription states that the town was founded by Tribeta, son of Linus, King of Assyria, and that Trèves was built before Rome. "Ante Roman Treveri statet, annis MCCC." The *Gesta Treverum* makes its history go back to the same founder. In further confirmation of this statement is the *Petrisberg* (the mountain of stone) and the same *Gesta* gives its old designation as the Mons Juranus or Jurano, which suggests the probability that, like the Tynwald and other British mounds, it was a seat of justice. It is a prehistoric circular mound, strikingly like one of our own British sacred mounds. Originally, this mound was probably surmounted by a menhir, which acted in the same way as the index, or gnomon, of a sundial. It was the writer's good fortune to see the sharp shadow of the solitary tree on the summit cast directly down the slopes of this mound of unknown antiquity as the great bell of the Dom-Kirche of St. Peter and St. Helen boomed the hour of noon. An object lesson which showed the value of Cotsworth's practical experiments on the summit of Silbury Hill, in order to verify his conviction that, like the Pyramids of Egypt, the "Cludair Cyvrangon" had been constructed by the astronomer-priests on astronomical lines.

Trèves is more closely connected with our early British monarchs than any other continental town, from its having been the favourite residence of the Queen-Empress Helena, who founded here the first Christian Church in Germany. The basilica of the palace of her husband, Constantine Chlorus, forms the actual walls of the present Cathedral. From her gifts of one of the nails of the Cross, of the Holy Coat, and other relics, the name of King Coel's beautiful and accomplished daughter "Elaine" is held in the greatest veneration as a patroness of the city. And it is of no little interest to find that the ruins of the imperial palace at Trèves, built by her son Constantine, bear so strong a resemblance to similar ruins in Colchester that postcards of the one may easily be taken for those of the other.

The Crimean War in the 'fifties of the last century afforded exceptional opportunity for comparing the present aspect of the Caucasian Cambria or Crimea with that handed down in the old British traditions. It is still what the latter describes it as being 3,500 years ago: the east of it covered by salt lagoons; a large portion occupied by the Sivash, or putrid, Sea; the rest composed of spits, reefs, and sandbanks. The southern part, which they called the Summer Land (Gwlad yr Hâv), is now known to richly merit the title. It is the Naples of the Russian Empire.

In the battles of the Alma and Inkermann and in the assaults on Sebastopol, more than 30,000 British Kymry in different regiments were engaged. It is a fact unparalleled in history that the descendants of a race which emigrated thirty-three centuries since, should thus return, to fight in the sacred cause of justice and civilization, to the cradle of their ancestors in the remote East, preserving the same language, the same freshness of life, the same indomitable spirit and endurance, the same innate attachment to liberty. Such an extraordinary instance of vitality in a nation appears to justify the faith of the Kymry in their popular proverb, "Tra mor, tra Brython"—"as long as there is sea, so long will there be Britons."

Geology enables us to determine that at the period of the Crimean colonization of Britain not more than half of it was inhabitable. The eastern parts, the lands adjoining the great estuaries of the Thames, Mersey, Humber, Trent, the Fen countries, were either submerged or mud-swamps. Many centuries elapsed before they became fit to support human life. The districts first settled were consequently the mountainous regions of the west and the elevated plateaus of the north and the south. Hence in Devonshire, Cornwall, Wales, Cumberland and the East of Scotland, are found the earliest works of man's hands in Britain—the circles, mounds, tumuli, and caerau, or fortified enclosures, of the three Pacific Tribes.

The patrimony of inheritance of the Elder Tribe, or Kymry, lay between the Severn and the sea; that of the Lloegreans extended from Kent to Cornwall; that of the Brythons stretched from the Humber northwards. The Kymry, gradually enlarging their bounds, colonized the north-west of the Isle, and the east of Albyn, or Scotland. These latter became known to the Romans as the Picts. All the names of the Pict kings, as of the rivers, mountains, etc., in Pictland, are Kymric.

The monarchic and military supremacy was vested in the Kymry. Strictly speaking, there appear to have been no laws, but the three tribes regulating their affairs by certain usages, which afterwards were called the Usages of Britain, and formed the foundations of its subsequent codes of law.

The whole Island was considered to be under one Crown— the Crown itself subject to the "Voice of the Country"; hence the maxim, "The Country is higher than the King," which runs through the Ancient British laws, and was directly opposed to the feudal system, in which the Country itself was dealt with as the property of the King.

The Kymric language prevailed in different dialects over the whole of Europe and a large part of Asia. It is the sub-structure of all the Keltic tongues and the Archaic element in the Greek, the Latin, the Sanskrit, and the hieroglyphic Egyptian (see Bunsen, *Christianity and Mankind*, vol. iv., p. 158). It is the key to the affinity between the languages of the East and the West. All other languages can be traced to an alien source—this alone cannot. It is certain it was brought by the Kymry into Britain, as it was spoken by their fore-fathers in Armenia 1700 B.C., and that its purity and integrity have been guarded by them in all ages with jealous care. It is the witness, alike above suspicion and corruption, to the extreme antiquity of their nationality and civilization.

The three Pacific Tribes remained undisturbed in the enjoy-ment of their several patrimonies in Britain for five centuries. A second colonization then took place on the breaking up of the Trojan Empire in the East. The Empire of Troy, its kings and people were of the same race and language as the Umbri of Italy and Britain. Hence on its dissolution part of the survivors directed their course to the former, part to the latter country. Troy was regarded as the sacred city of the race in the East.

The only two national names acknowledged by the Ancient Britons are Kymry and Y Lin Troia, the race of Troy. There seems no sufficient reason therefore to doubt the traditional story that Brutus, having accidentally killed his father in the chase, and being ordered by his grandfather Æneas to quit Italy, assembled three thousand of the bravest youths of Umbria, and putting himself at their head, sailed to his countrymen in Greece. A series of victories on the Trojan side resulted in peace; Pandrasus giving his daughter Imogene in marriage to Brutus. But, finding that a Trojan kingdom could not be established in Albania (afterwards called Epirus), except at the cost of incessant hostilities, Brutus emigrated with all his people to the mainstock of his race—the White Island. Drayton, the Elizabethan poet, gives an account of the wanderings of Æneas after the destruction of Troy and relates the expulsion of Brutus from Italy and his ultimate arrival in the

". . . Isle of Albion highly bless'd
With giants lately stored. . . .
Where from the stock of Troy, those puissant kings should rise
Whose conquests from the West, the world should scant suffice."

Spenser also in the *Faerie Queene* refers to "Noble Britons sprung from Trojans bold" and to Brutus having given the name of Troja Nova to London. We have the testimony also of the early British historians Gildas and Nennius, the Welsh "Bruts," Matt. Paris and other writers in support of the tradition. But perhaps the most ancient documentary evidence of the foundation of London is to be found in a Latin chronicle, in which Edward the Confessor speaks of London as "fundata olim et edificata ad instar magna Troje," which, translated, runs thus: a city founded and built after the likeness of Great Troy.

Tradition says that on his journey to the "White Island" Brutus touched at Melita (Malta) and, coasting along the southern shore of the Mediterranean, he gave the coast the name of Mauritania, which it still retains. They then steered through the Straits of Libyan Hercules (Gibraltar) into the Atlantic, then called the Tyrrhenian Ocean. Upon the southern coast of Spain they came across four other Trojan colonies, under Trœnius. These were readily persuaded to join them. The combined expeditions sailed northwards, and anchored off the mouth of the Loire. The great plain between the Alps and the Atlantic had by this time been thickly peopled by the descendants of the Alpine and Auvergnian Kymry; these called themselves Kelts or Gael, and the country Gaul or Gallia. The King of the Gael was Goffar. Brutus, advancing through Gascony, threw up his camp in the centre of Goffar's domains. An engagement was fought, in which Tyrrhi, Brutus' nephew was killed. In honour of him he built an immense tumulus where now stands the city, called, after Tyrrhi, Tours. Goffar being completely defeated, the fleet repaired and re-victualled, sailed the next year round

91

the Horn of Armorica and finally anchored off Talnus in Torbay.

It is at Totnes on the Dart, twelve miles inland from Torbay, the oldest seaport in South Devon, that we find the surest proof of the personality of Brutus in a custom handed down from time immemorial, and last observed May 6, 1910, when the Mayor read the Proclamation of King George standing upon a granite boulder embedded in the pavement of the principal street (Fore Street) leading up the steep ascent from the river to the Westgate of the town. Over this venerable relic hangs a sign inscribed "This is Brutus' Stone," the tradition being that on this stone the Trojan prince set foot, when he landed in Britain some few years after the fall of Troy, 1185 B.C.

In the Welsh records it is stated that the three Pacific Tribes received their countrymen from the East as brethren; Brutus was proclaimed king, and at a national convention of the whole Island, with its dependencies, was elected Sovereign Paramount. The throne of Hu Gadarn thus devolved upon him both by descent and suffrage. His three sons, born after his arrival in Britain, he named after the three Pacific Tribes, Locrinus, Camber and Alban. Brutus' name heads the roll in all the genealogies of the British kings, preserved as faithfully as were those of the kings of Israel and Judah.

The descent of the British kings from Brutus was never disputed for fifteen hundred years. The "Island of Brutus" was the common name of the Island in old times. The word *tan* is the old British term for *land*; Brutannia (pronounced Britannia, the British "u" being sounded as "e") is Brut's or Brutus' Land. The term is also of very ancient use in Asia, as Beluchistan, Afghanistan. The Trojan descent is said to solve all the peculiarities in British Laws and Usages which would otherwise be wholly inexplicable.

Whether the Tot, or sacred mound, which has given its name to the town and the neighbouring shores was in existence when Brutus landed, it is impossible to say. From the organized reception accorded to the Trojan prince, it is probable that the "Holy Hill" had been "piled up" by the neolithic settlers of a previous migration, who have left many similar traces of their religious monuments, on the plateaus of Dartmoor, on the Wiltshire downs, and elsewhere. The Tot is an entirely artificial mound of the average dimensions of these prehistoric Gorsedds—namely, 100 feet in diameter at the base, diminishing to about 80 feet at the top. The Great Seat stands on the highest point of the hill, commanding the town. Round about its base lie the ruins of the Norman castle. The summit of the mound itself is enclosed with a stone wall, and, like the round Table Mound at Windsor, has never been roofed in. From the summit a magnificent view is obtained: looking south one sees a long straight reach of the river set among the hills, up which the salt tide is pouring from Dartmouth, so rapidly that it grows wider every moment. Northeast, from out of the haze loom the rugged Tors of Dartmoor; whilst westward, roll in endless billows the forest-clad hills of Devon and Cornwall.

The trees and underwood that now clothe the Tot have almost obliterated the terraced lines of its original contour, similar to those on Silbury, and other mounds of the same character that have not been planted, lines which only the scientific investigations of our own day have shown were drawn with such consummate skill by the ancient astronomers that by using these as sighting lines, the warning star of sunrise could be observed and the times and seasons fixed.

That the Tot preserved its traditions as a Gorsedd, i.e. *a Great Seat or throne of the Monarch*, from Kymric to Norman times we have historic proof in the fact that William of Normandy erected a castle, under the shadow of the mound, and gave it to one Judhael, who is said to have been a Breton, whose contingent of Bretons are reputed to have won for the Conqueror the field of Senlac, so eager were they to retaliate on the foes of their race, the Saxon. Totnes is thus referred to in Domesday: "Judhael holds of the King the Borough of Totnes, which King Edward the Confessor held in his demesne." William Rufus, it is recorded, expelled Judhael de Totnes out of his inheritance. King John gave the keeping of the Castle to Henry, son of the Earl of Cornwall. Its romantic history onwards we have no space to relate. In 1645 the Castle was in possession of the King's forces. At the present time a few old walls are all that remain of the royal Castle. The property belongs to the Duke of Somerset, in whose family it appears to have been since the Stuart times.

Neither in Keltic literature nor in tradition have we been able to find any mention of the movements of Brutus immediately after he had been proclaimed King Paramount at Totnes. It is probable he lost no time in making his way to the headquarters of Kymric administration, the Metropolitical Temple of the "Mighty Ones," Abury or Avebury, and that within the supreme Gorsedd, the chosen of the People was first "lifted"[1] by the Elders to a stone sedd or seat according to a most ancient custom of the Kymry, and there crowned within the precincts of the stone circle, in the presence of a vast concourse assembled on the Earth-circle (a mile in circumference) that enclosed the Temples of the sun and moon, the only portion, alas! of this majestic prehistoric monument that was not destroyed in the wreckage of the eighteenth century.

That Stonehenge was standing at this time is no longer an uncertainty, thanks to Sir Norman Lockyer's observations and calculations, taken from the precincts of the Solar Circle, which have proved the "Circle of the Dominion" to have been erected *circa* 1680 B.C., some five centuries before the fall of Troy in 1185 B.C., and the subsequent dispersion of the Trojans. These dates may possibly help us to identify the personalities of the mysterious "7 Old Kings" and "7 New Kings," whose barrows may be seen on the horizon from the Great Circle of the Ambresbiri. The tumuli of the "7 Old Kings" may be the burial mounds of the monarchs of Hu Gadarn's migration, who each in his day had been "lifted" and "crowned" within the northern circle of the "Potentes," under the shadow of the mighty mound of the Cludair Cyvrangon whose age, like that of the Temple of Abury, will probably never be known.

And may not the barrows of the "7 New Kings" contain the mortal remains of the successors of Brutus, of the heroic

---

[1] Richard II was the last king who was "lifted" to the stone seat, which down to the time that the Houses of Parliament and St. Stephen's Chapel were burnt, 1833, was at the upper end of Westminster Hall.

Trojan race, destined, as they believed, to sway a wider Empire than either the Asiatic or Italian Troy (Rome)—a tradition which some hope is in the course of fulfilment?

In the Chronicles it is stated that "Brutus, minded to build him a chief city, went round the whole circuit of the land in search of a fitting site. When he came to the river Thames he found the very spot best suited to the purpose. He therefore founded his city there and called it New Troy, and by this name it was known for many ages thereafter until at last, by corruption of the word, it came to be called Trinovantum."

A glance at the index of an atlas shows that London was not the only city in Europe to have been called after the historic Troy; there are two towns of that name in Italy and one in France. In the ancient Troy on the Tagus, although practically destroyed by the earthquake, many remains of so-called Phœnician masonry may still be seen. In our own case we have to account for the loss of the name of Troy before the Roman invasion in 52 B.C. The solution of the difficulty may be that the older prehistoric name of the Llandin triumphed over the alien appellation of Caer Troia.

Brutus' knowledge of the different seaports of the Mediterranean would have led him at once to appreciate the exceptional capabilities of the site of the Kymric Caer, perched on a hillock on the narrowest reach of a tidal river, with two natural ports, the Walbrook and the Fleet, and practically impregnable by land, girt in as it was by primeval forest on the north, by fen and moor on the east and west and unapproachable from the south, the shore from Battersea and Greenwich being one unbroken expanse of mud some 8 miles long, varying from 2 to 2½ in width, twice in every twenty-four hours submerged by the tide.

The numerous prehistoric remains unearthed in the city and figured in the catalogue of the Guildhall Museum afford positive proof of a Neolithic occupation, succeeded by that of the Bronze Age. The evidence of these material remains point to the probability that the original settlers were no other than the first wave of emigrant under Hu Gadarn, the mounds and circle-builders of Britain.

Seeing that the great waterway of the Severn had its

Glastonbury and its Caerleon, and the South Coast its Totnes and its Winton, it is most unlikely that the site of London would have been neglected from the coming of Hu Gadarn in the time of Abraham, to the arrival of Brutus and his Trojans in the days of Samuel, unique as it is, in position as the only high ground on the North Bank of the Thames, 60 miles from the sea. Navigable, moreover, for nearly its entire length of 150 miles, the prehistoric mounds of Windsor, Wallingford and Oxford testify to the existence of early Kymric settlements on the banks of this all-important waterway on the East of the Island.

Brutus is celebrated in the Triads as one of the "Three King Revolutionists of Britain," the Trojan system under him being incorporated with the Patriarchal. The changes which the Trojan Prince intended to carry out may have influenced his choice in making the Porth of the Llandin his capital, a trading centre, removed from the immediate influence of the Druidic authorities at Abury, who would, naturally, have resented any innovation of their own ancient laws. It is satisfactory to find the text of the Triad confirmed by the most learned jurists, who refer the original Institutes of our Island to the Trojan law brought by Brutus. Lord Chief Justice Cope (Preface to Vol. III of Report) affirms "the original laws of this land were composed of such elements as Brutus first selected from the Ancient Greek and Trojan institutions."

It is to these native laws, says Morgan, and "not as has been absurdly alleged to any foreign or continental source, German, Saxon or Norman, Britons have in all ages been indebted," for the superior liberties they have enjoyed as contrasted with other nations. Lord Chancellor Fortescue, in his work on the Laws of England, justly observes, "Concerning the different powers which kings claim over their subjects, I am firmly of opinion that it arises solely from the different nature of the original institutions. So the kingdom of Britain had its original from Brutus of the Trojans, who attended him from Italy and Greece and wove a mixed government, compounded of the regal and democratic."

The most memorable of the laws of Brutus is that of the

Royal Primogeniture, by which the succession to the Throne of Britain was vested in the eldest son of the King. This was known as pre-eminently "the Trojan law," and has in all ages regulated the succession to the British Crown among the British dynasties. It was eventually adopted by the Normans and became the law of England. Another fundamental ordinance established by Brutus was, that the sovereigns of Cambria and Alban should be so far subordinate to the sovereign of Llœgria that they should pay him annually forty pounds weight of gold, for the military and naval defence of the Island. The whole Island was never to be regarded otherwise than one Kingdom and One Crown. This Crown was called "the Crown of Britain" and the sovereignty over the whole Island vested in it—the Crownship of Britain, *Unbennaeth Prydain.* The military leadership remained in the Eldest Tribe, the Kymry, and from it the *Pendragon,* or military dictator, with absolute power for the time being, was, in the case of foreign invasion or national danger, to be elected. The leadership was the same as Sparta exercised in Greece and Rome in Italy. Every subject was as free as the King. There were no other laws in force than those which were known as *Cyfreithiau,* or "Common Rights." There were no slaves, the first slaves in aftertimes were the *Caethion,* or captives taken in war.

The Usages of Britain could not be altered, by any act of the Crown or National Convention. They were now considered the inalienable rights to which every Briton was born, and of which no human legislation could deprive him. Many of these usages are remarkable for their humane and lofty spirit, for instance, "There are three things belonging to a man, from which no law can separate him—his wife, his children and the instruments of his calling, for no law can unman a man, or uncall a calling."

A British or Trojan law remains in full force to this day— that the sceptre of the Island might be swayed by a queen as well as a king. In the Pict kingdom, the succession went wholly by the female side. Amongst the continental nations no woman was permitted to reign, the Saxons considered it a disgrace to a king to be seen seated on a throne with a queen.

The chariot system of warfare and the system of military castrametation are said to have been introduced into Britain by Brutus. Cæsar describes both as having attained, in his time, the highest perfection. The British castrametation was, in some important respects, superior to the Roman.

Another memory of the Trojan colonization is perpetuated in the numerous Troy Towns or Mazes cut in the turf in all parts of England and in those which still exist in the uplands of Wales, called by the shepherds "Caerdroia," the city of Troy, allusion to which is made in *Drych y Prif Oesoedd* and in other Welsh histories. There is nothing more popular among the Welsh, we are told, than the belief that they came originally into this island from Caerdroia. This tradition has impressed itself so indelibly on the Keltic mind, that we see even shepherds on the summit of every hillock making pictorial representations in the surface of the grass of the labyrinthine walls of ancient Troy. On the plains on both sides of the Solway, mazes are also to be met with, and as in Wales herdsmen still cut labyrinthine figures upon the turf, which they call, for no reason except that their fathers used the same expression, the "Wall of Troy."

Whether the name Troy Town was used generically of all turf-cut mazes, it is impossible to say, but it is certain that many of them in different parts of the country were so designated, and both in name and in form take us back to classical antiquity. Even around London the name survives; for example, at Peckham Rye an old row of cottages built on the site which formed part of the Common is called Troy Town. The upper garden at Kensington was known as the "Siege of Troy"; it was on this site William III laid out a topiary maze, and at about the same time he restored Henry VIII's popular maze at Hampton Court, which that monarch may have probably founded upon a yet earlier maze of unknown antiquity.

At Blackheath another maze may be identified in the midst of the prehistoric remains, where, not far from the entrance to Morden College, successive ridges and depressions, faintly discernible, represent the remains of the old labyrinthine pathway. An old survey of the Manor of Greenwich shows that the familiar thoroughfare of Maze Hill led direct to the Maze. That this commanding tableland was an important centre of civilization in remote antiquity is certain from the partial remains of the prehistoric Gorsedd (Great Seat) to-day known as Whitfield's Mount, where, as upon similar sites in the vicinity of London previously described, the "Privelege" of the people to hold public meetings still survives, and it is only within the memory of the present generation that the numerous barrows, which for centuries crowned the Lansdown (Llan, *sacred*) and the Point, commanding the river for some six miles on the east and west, as also the upper part of the royal Park, have been ruthlessly destroyed in order to supply the ever-increasing demands for cricket and football grounds.

Passing right through the middle of these tumuli on the Heath ran Watling Street, the old trade route from the South Coast to the Porth of the Llandin. Its north-westerly course has been traced on the high ground near Peckham, where, as we have seen, was another Troy Town, probably connected with the "Place of Assembly," the Sacred Mound at Kenning-*ton*. The names of Maze Pond, Maze Street, and Maze Lane, near the site of the old Ferry on Bankside, Southwark (Wark, fortification), preserve the memory of yet another of these places of amusement, as some suppose them to have been, and suggest the presence of a large population, composed probably of traders and merchants connected with the control of the corn supplies from the numerous "dene holes," or granaries, in Kent and Surrey, for it was at this point that food and other commodities were conveyed into the old Caer of *New Troy*.

The Ferry at Southwark would appear to have rivalled the ford at Westminster in importance, from the fact that before a stone of the Abbey was laid, we find St. Swithin, Bishop of Winchester, in the ninth century buying up the site of the ferry and building his beautiful cathedral, to which he attached a college for the training of secular priests to minister to the spiritual needs of the people, as well as to administer civic justice. It is to the first Chancellor-Bishop St. Swithin that the country owes the first organized attempt to re-

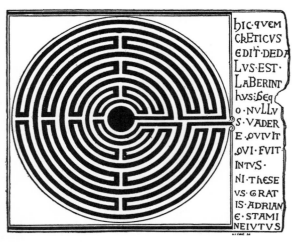

hIC·QVEM
CRETICVS
EDIT·DEDA
LVS·EST·
LABERINT
hVS:SEQ
o·NVLLV
S·VADER
E·QVIVIT
QVI·FVIT
INTVS·
NI·ThESE
VS·GRAT
IS·ADRIAN
E·STAMI
NEIVTVS

MAZE IN LUCCA CATHEDRAL

100

establish the Druidic system of Church and State government on Christian lines, a system peculiar to Britain, with the traditions of which the Bishop would have become acquainted in royal Winchester, where his Cathedral stood on the actual site of a Druidic Court of Justice. It has been thought, moreover, that it was the Druidic College of Priests in the Close that suggested to St. Swithin to found Theological Colleges at Winchester and Southwark. Be this as it may, on the north side of the sacristy of Southwark Cathedral the remains of the Saxon apse are said to exist, and marking the work of St. Swithin as the first Chancellor-Bishop of England is the original stone seat on the north-east side of the Chancel, where, for centuries, Bishops of Winchester held their Consistory Courts.

Not only was the great St. Swithin the founder of secular education in Saxon times, but it is to the Chancellor-Bishop, the Church owes the revival and restoration by statute of the Druidic law of tithes. The terrible incursions and depredations of the Danes, the Bishop regarded as a visitation of Providence for the neglect and poverty into which the Churches in all parts of the country had been allowed to fall from the lack of funds and dearth of clergy. It was to remedy the latter need that he established his Seminary at Winchester, the "Nurserie" of his College at Southwark, and in order to alleviate the former, King Ethelwulf by his Chancellor's advice "booked" (gebochde) the tenth part of the land of the kingdom to God's praise and his own eternal welfare. The deed was written at Winchester (from early British times to Edward III the seat of government) and laid solemnly on the altar of the Cathedral Church in presence of Swithin and the Witan—the Saxon Parliament. It was thus by consent of Church and State that the payment of tithes became established as a national institution. The original Charter is in the British Museum, written in the year 854, with the consent of those witnesses whose names and signatures are attached.

To go further afield, in addition to the mazes at Blackheath, Peckham Rye and Southwark, there is Troy Town at Rochester, adjoining an open space called the Vines; Troy Town, $3\frac{1}{4}$ miles from Dorchester, a maze at Leigh between

Yetminster and Yeovil; Wick Down at Downton; Breame Down near Salisbury; St. Ann's, Sneinton, Notts.; another near Ripon; Comberton in Cambridgeshire; Caerleon in Monmouthshire, and the maze at Somerton, near Oxford, known to this day as Troy Town or Troy Farm. Ruskin compares the design of this Oxfordshire turf-cut Troy Town, or maze, to the circular labyrinth of Dædalus depicted on a stone in Lucca Cathedral, and he is the first to call attention to the fact that it closely resembles the circular labyrinth on a coin of Knossos in Crete. But the three most interesting examples are Saffron Walden maze, which occupies a space of 138 feet by 100, while the convolutions of its path are said to measure about a mile in length; the maze on the Winton (*sacred mound*), St. Catherine's Hill, Winchester; and the Alkborough Maze, commanding the Humber on the borders of Lincolnshire, known as Julian's Bower. It is a curious coincidence that the design of these three existing mazes should belong respectively to the types seen on the coins of Crete, casts of which have been kindly given to the author for reproduction, by Mr. G. F. Hill of the Coin and Medal Department, British Museum.

This is no chance resemblance, but has behind it the fact attested by Virgil that the Trojans came from Crete (*Æneid* iii. 90).

Stukeley tells us that the Maze at Alkborough, in Lincolnshire, used to be known within his own recollection as "Julian's Bower," and he adds that the same name was applied to many other mazes then existing on village greens. The word Bower in place-names is a corruption of Burgh, a castle or city. Julian is probably no other than Julius or Iulus, the son of Æneas of Troy. Julian's Bower is therefore the "City of Iulus," which may be taken as the equivalent of Troy Town.

The names of Troy Town and Julian's Bower, applied to our ancient English mazes, were treated in uncritical times as "confirmation strong as Holy Writ" of the descent of the Ancient Britons from Brutus and his Trojan followers. However much this tradition may be questioned there must have been some reason for associating these turf-cut labyrinths on our downs and commons with the city of Priam and the connecting link may perhaps be found in the Roman game of Troy.

An animated description of the Troy Game is given in the *Æneid*, book v, in a passage in which Virgil professes to afford an account of its origin:

"Father Æneas commands all the throning people to draw back from the long Circus and that the plain should be clear. The youthful warriors advance and in even line glitter on their bridle steeds before their fathers' eyes: as they pass by all the youth of Troy and Sicily admire and cheer. The hair of all is restrained according to rule by garlands of slipped leaves; they bear two shafts of Cornel wood tipped with steel; some wear polished quivers on their shoulders; high on the breast a bent circlet of twisted gold runs round their neck. Three troops of horse and three leaders gallop hither and thither; twelve youths follow each captain and shine in divided bands under leaders of equal bodies, and each of the three squadrons broke up its companies with parted bands and again at a signal they wheeled around and charged with levelled spear. They then made charges and retreats to and fro, still opposite to one another, and they interlock hither and thither their wheeling circles, and in arms present the image of a battle; and now they expose their backs in flight, now charge with spear, and now make peace and ride abreast.

"As in days of old, the Labyrinth in lofty Crete is said to have possessed a way, enmeshed 'mid baffling walls and the tangled mystery of a thousand paths, that there, a trickery, that none could grasp, and whence was no return, might destroy the clue of progress; just so the sons of Troy entangle their paths at a gallop, and interweave flight and combat in sport; like dolphins who, as they swim through the waters of the sea, cleave the Carpathian and Libyan deep and gambol through the waves. This mode of exercise and these contests first did Ascanius revive, when he girdled Alba Longa with walls, and taught our Latin forefathers to celebrate after the fashion in which he himself when a boy, and with him the Trojan youth, had celebrated them. The Albans taught their sons and from them mighty Rome received the games in due course and cherished the ancestral custom, and even now the game is called Troy, and the boys are called the Trojan band. Thus far were the games celebrated in honour of the holy sire of Æneas."

This account of Virgil's produces the impression of a

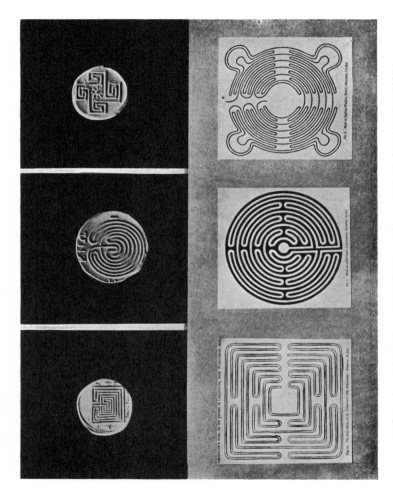

MAZES AT WINCHESTER, ALKBOROUGH, LINCS., AND SAFFRON WALDEN, ESSEX, SHOWING RESEMBLANCE TO COINS OF KNOSSOS bewildering complexity of movement upon clearly formulated lines, and it must be admitted that there is a striking coincidence in the fact that on the one hand we find Virgil describing the Troy Game as consisting of movements which are only comparable to the entangled pathways of the labyrinth or maze of Crete; and that, on the other hand, we find our ancient turf-cut mazes so commonly known down even to our own time as Troy Towns or Walls of Troy. The coincidence becomes all the more remarkable when we see how Virgil connects Iulus or Julius with the Troy Game, and recall that Julian's Bower, that is Julian's Castle or City, is another name given to our old English mazes.

The story of the Cretan Labyrinth referred to by Virgil, in illustration of the "entangled" and "interwoven" figures of the Troy Game, is familiar even in our nurseries. The skilful workman Dædalus constructed for King Minos a labyrinth, in the centre of which the Minotaur had his lair. No one who entered this labyrinth could find his way out again. The seven young men and maidens who formed the annual tribute of Athens were sent into the Maze, lost themselves in its winding passages, and were devoured by the monster. Theseus slew the Minotaur and escaped out of the labyrinth by the help of the clue which Ariadne had given him.

But what had the Cretan legend to do with Troy?

It is material to recall that Ilium was supposed to have been founded by settlers from Crete. Virgil tells us in the *Æneid*, that Crete was the cradle of the Trojan race and the source of its national religion. Virgil is understood to have based his poem upon mythical histories which have since altogether disappeared, and it may be assumed that the ethnical connexion of Troy with Crete was an accepted belief in the age in which he wrote. Thus it is possible that the story of the Minotaur may have been regarded as a legend of the Trojan people, and the famous labyrinth may have been associated in the popular mind with Troy as well as Crete.

Again it must be remembered that Troy had a legend of its own which bore a strong resemblance to that of Crete. The story was that Neptune and Apollo appeared in the guise of men before Laomedon, King of Troy, and undertook, for an agreed price, to build a wall round the city. When the task was accomplished, Laomedon refused to pay them. Thereupon, Neptune sent a marine monster, which was wont to issue forth from the water into the fields of Ilium, seizing and devouring the inhabitants. An oracle declared that in order to appease the angry god it was necessary for Laomedon to expose his daughter, Hesione, upon the shore, that the monster might devour her. Hesione was accordingly taken forth, but Hercules came to her rescue and undertook to destroy the monster. In order to assist him in his enterprise, Minerva built for him a wall of earth, behind which he would retire "when the sea monster from the shore unto the plain would chase him" (see xx. Il. 145; Deod. iv. 42; Apollod. ii. 5–9).

It is to this story that Shakespeare refers in *The Merchant of Venice*, Act III, Scene 2:

> "with much more love
> Than young Alcides, when he did reduce
> The virgin tribute paid by howling Troy
> To the sea monster."

The Rev. R. L. Morgan, in his *History of the Kymri*, referring to Laomedon, says that in the reign of the latter "the citadel and walls of Troy were rebuilt by Belin and Lêv, architects of Crete, after the model of the Cretan labyrinth, which was also an exact representation of the stellar universe." This interesting statement must not be omitted, although at present Science has neglected to prove its claims.

Reference is also made to the Walls of Troy by Lydgate in his *Troy Book*, where he speaks of Brutus, who won Britain from the giants. Chaucer, Caxton, Denham, Milton, all refer to the story of Brutus.

This legend is rather alluded to than related by Homer and other writers whose works have come down to us. It is taken for granted by authorities in classical literature that a more complete and detailed narrative than we possess existed and was familiar to the ancients. One wonders whether, if the full story were before us, we should find that the analogy to the Cretan legend was carried out and that Minerva's walls were

labyrinth in their form. Even without this added circumstance is it possible that the charging and retreating, the
chasing and eluding, which seem to have characterized the
combat between Hercules and the Trojan monster, were
sufficient to suggest the name of Troy Game as descriptive of
the mock combat of the Roman youths? The game may have
been designated without any special reference to the labyrinthine movements of which it consisted.

In London, in the days of Henry II, FitzStephen relates
that Troy Game was played by the young men of the King's
household every Sunday in Lent, the King and his courtiers
frequently being present. Troy Game on horse-back con-
tinued to be played down to the Middle Ages and was probably the origin of jousts and tournaments, afterwards so
popular. We have come across more than one reference to its
having been played on Tothill Fields.

Mimic warfare between opposing companies of schoolboys
might very naturally be named after the immortal combats
that formed one of the principal subjects of their lessons.
Even in modern English playgrounds the game of Greeks and
Trojans still holds its place with French and English, and few
among us realize that the game of Troy is still played in our
streets under the name of "Hop Scotch." Intricate lines are
drawn on the pavement in chalk and competitors try to reach
the goal by devious ways. As to the origin of the word Maze,
it is from a Kymric word *maes*, meaning greensward in the
Cornish language=a *field*; the name seems to indicate that in
some bygone age, the maze game was played on the greensward. We still use the word *maze* and *amazement* to express
the bewilderment of one who knows not which way to turn.

But to return to the story of the Trojan prince, the founder
of London.

Brutus died after a memorable reign of twenty-four years
and was interred by the side of Imogene on the Bryn Gwyn
(the White Mount). The genealogies record the names of the
British kings, Brutus, descendants and successors, but it is
not mentioned that any of these monarchs were buried on the
Royal Gorsedd until Dunwal Molmutius in the fourth century
B.C., whose history we shall learn later.

Brutus was succeeded in Llœgria by his eldest son Locrinus, in Albyn by his second son, Alban, and in Cambria by his youngest son, Camber. The portion of Britain assigned to Trœnius, the valiant companion of Brutus, was the Western Keryn, or promontory, extending from Torbay to the Land's End, part of which is now known as Cornwall. From the Keryn, Trœnius changed his name into Keryn or Corineus. The Dukedom of Cornwall thus founded was a Dukedom Royal, that is the Duke within it exercised the same prerogatives as the Kings of Llœgria, Cambria and Albyn did within their territories. Next to these crowns, it is the oldest title in Britain. Spenser alludes to this naming of Cornwall in the *Faerie Queene*:

> "In meed of these great conquests by them gott,
> Corineus had that province utmost west
> To him assigned for his worthy lott,
> Which of his name and memorable gest,
> He called Cornwaile."

The tradition that a race of giants dwelt in Cornwall, Drayton quaintly alludes to in his *Polyolbion*. After a terrible struggle, the Trojans got the upper hand and killed all their assailants, except the leader, Goemagot who was preserved for combat with Corineus, who, "holding it a diversion to encounter giants," met him on a spot pointed out to this day on Plymouth Hoe. Goemagot broke three of his opponent's ribs and this so enraged Corineus that, taking the giant upon his shoulders, he ran with him to the shore and getting upon the top of a high rock, hurled the savage monster into the sea. The struggle between these mighty men of valour was recorded as late as Queen Elizabeth's time, by what Carew calls the "pourtradture of two men with clubbes in their hands cut in the turf, the one bigger, the other lesser, whom they term Gogmagog and Corineus, intimating the wrestling to have been between these two champions and the steep rocky cliff affording aptitude for such a cast." Carew considers that the great activity of Devon and Cornishmen in the faculty of wrestling seems to "derive them a speciall pedigree from that grand wrastler Corineus."

Spenser in his *Faerie Queene*, where he records the early history of Britain, refers to the conflict of Brutus and Corineus with the giants.

> "But ere he had established his throne
> And spread the empire to the utmost shore,
> He fought great battles, with his savage foes,
> In which he defeated evermore,
> And many giants left on groaning flore,
> That well can witness yet unto this day.
> The Western Hough, besprinkled with the gore
> Of mighty Goemagot, whom in stout play
> Corineus conqered and cruelly did slay."

The Plymouth Corporation records confirm the recutting and renewal of these figures as early as 1494. It was only when the citadel was erected in 1671 that this interesting monument was destroyed. The story of Jack the Giant Killer is said to have had its origin in the combat of Corineus with the Cornish giant and there seems little reason to doubt the tradition that the two gigantic figures in the Guildhall of the City of London, popularly called Gog and Magog, really present Corineus and Goemagot.

And now in the light gathered from similar mounds in other parts of Britain, we will pass on to a more detailed examination of the prehistoric mounds that stood round about the Porth of the Llandin (or the Lyndin=the Lake City) the Caer Troia of Brutus, the Londin or Londinium of the Romans. Upon the two natural eminences of the Llandin and the Penton, the eyes of Brutus must have rested when he made choice of the Kymric Caer for his capital; the two smaller artificial mounds of the Bryn Gwyn and the Tothill may have been erected by the Trojan king as trade increased under his rule. It is conceivable that in the foreknowledge of the Creator, the two "high-places" commanding the marshes, east, west and south may have been predestined to be used in the service of the Lord of Hosts, as Holy Hills from whose summits the astronomer-priests, in the dawn of civilization, might study the "heavens," that "declare the Glory of God" and the firmament that "sheweth his handiwork"; and by heliograph, semaphore or beacon light, signal the time and the seasons, the result of their observations for the daily direction of the lives of the traders and sea-faring population of the Porth. History has proved the wisdom of Brutus' choice of what appeared a very unpromising district for a capital, which has held its own and won its way to the foremost place, as the capital of the British Empire and the greatest city in the world.

The Llandin—Parliament Hill—is the largest, loftiest and most imposing of the four prehistoric "Gorsedds of *Great Seats*" of the Metropolis. Standing on a spur of the Northern Heights in an amphitheatre of wooded hills midway between Hampstead and Highgate, from its site and surroundings the *Sacred Eminence* retains somewhat of its original dignity as a "high-place of worship." The structure of the hill is London clay at its base, gradually changing to a sandy loam. The central boss would appear to have been sculptured from the highest layer, since there is a circular terrace still distinct. Half a century ago, the sighting lines (somewhat similar to those on Silbury) and graded slopes were to be traced, but a pathway over the summit and trees planted on the sides have destroyed the original contour; a vestige of the trench remains, which in Kymric times encircled the base, but the spring has been diverted by the L.C.C., and now forms a series of ponds where bathing and boating may be enjoyed by the general public. Symbolic, as are all our prehistoric mounds, of the earth rising out of the sea, a British Gorsedd may always be known by its symbolic trench.

Parliament Hill carries on its Keltic traditions as a place of assembly to this day. On the north-eastern slope is a stone monument on which an inscription states that here public speaking is allowed. The numerous assemblies, religious and political, which from time immemorial have been held either on the mound itself or on "Parliament Fields" at its base, is an interesting survival of a national custom.

The Llandin has been called the "Areopagus" of Britain, from the tradition that St. Paul preached from the summit. On this account the Apostle became the Patron Saint of London, and his emblem, the sword of martyrdom, incorporated in the arms of the City, in the same way as St. Peter became the Patron Saint of Chartres from the tradition that this Apostle preached in the "Grotte des Druides," the Druidic rock temple, the actual foundations of the oldest Cathedral in France.

What is more likely if, as history tells us, St. Paul's friends were the children of Caractacus, than they should take measures for the conversion of their native land? And the great love St. Paul had for his peculiar mission to the Gentile world would not have allowed him to overlook the claims of such an important city as the "Colonia Augusta" of the Roman writers.

The Roman historian, Tacitus, writing in A.D. 61, describes Londinium as famous for its vast number of merchants who resorted to it for its widely-extended commerce and for the abundance of every species of commodity which it could supply. Strabo speaks of British merchants as bringing to the Seine and the Rhine shiploads of corn and cattle, iron, hides, slaves and dogs, and taking back brass, ivory, amber ornaments, and vessels of glass. And that the Port was considered by the Romans as the Metropolis of Britain is further established by the fact of its being the residence of the Vicar of Britain. The abode of such an officer clearly marks London to have been a Seat of Government, of Justice, and of the administration of the finances which consequently contributed to its extent, its magnificence and its wealth. "As early as the year A.D. 359, eight hundred vessels were employed for the conveyance and exportation of corn only," says Brayley in his *Londinium*.

The prehistoric burial-ground of the leaders of pre-Roman times was close around Parliament Hill, reminding us of the cemetery round about Silbury. Several barrows remain to this day, notably Primrose Hill and Barrow Hill, the site to-day of a reservoir. Other tumuli have been levelled and all trace of them lost. A bird's-eye view of the two cities, one in Britain and one in Asia Minor, would offer a general resemblance, and in the case of the latter the tombs bear the names of the heroes of the Trojan war, as every tourist will remember.

At Highgate a memorial of the national religion survives in the place-names of the Grove and Bishopswood. Situated on high ground, on the fringe of the forest that in Kymric times framed the Gorsedd, the Grove commands a view of both Parliament Hill and the Penton, and was the probable site of the Druidic College where dwelt the "ministers of law and order"—the Druids. Bishopswood (mainly consisting of oak trees) lies at the foot of a steep descent westward of the Grove and is so called from the fact that it has formed, from time immemorial, part of the endowment of the Bishopric of London. There is documentary evidence of the Emperor Constantine having bestowed the royal demesnes hereabouts and a portion of the Forest on the diocese of London, together with the Gorsedd lands of "King Coel's" castle in Cunobeline's royal city of Camulodunum; Colchester being at that time in the diocese of London. Constantine thus appears to have followed in the footsteps of his predecessors Arviragus at Glastonbury, and Lucius at Winchester, in thus transferring the Druidic emoluments of the Gorsedds to the maintenance of the Christian faith, now established as the national religion.

In Triad III, § 62, special mention is made of the Emperor Constantine. He is, according to the Triad, the first of the Emperors to extend his royal patronage to those who assembled together in the Faith of Christ. It is noteworthy this mention is connected with the three Archbishops of the Island of Britain.

At the foot of Parliament Hill is Gospel Oak Station, a name which connects the Druidic with the Christian religion, and links British and Saxon customs. One of the first acts of Edward the Confessor after his coronation at Winchester was to renew the Charter of Rights to the citizens of London, seated under the sacred oak of the Druids.

The Penton (Pen signifying in Keltic a hill rounded like a head) is a natural height about halfway between the Llandin and the Bryn Gwyn. The New River reservoir now occupies the site of the prehistoric sanctuary, and its massive masonry and earthworks have completely obliterated all traces of the original circular contour of the Ton (sacred mound). Approached by mean streets, nothing could well be more dismal and depressing than the appearance of this prehistoric Gorsedd as we see it to-day. It is difficult even to imagine it as depicted by Hollar, still less as the spot where, in Elizabethan times, Gerard the herbalist mentions he found the "white saxifrage growing in abundance." But if the beautiful greensward has disappeared and the Penton has lost its rural aspect, there is the same far-stretching panoramic view to be seen, as in British times, however much it may differ in detail. It is well worth a pilgrimage if only to appreciate the magnificent site of the "Holy Hill," and to gaze on the splendour of the "dim rich City" spread out at our feet with its mysterious medley of spires, domes and palaces, dominated by St. Paul's, gleaming from out the mist, like some beautiful vision. No site could have better realized in its day the regulations laid down by Aedd Mawr, the founder of the Druidic Order, viz. that a "Gorsedd of the Bards of Britain must be held on a green spot, in a conspicuous place in full view and hearing of country and aristocracy, in the face of the sun, the eye of Light, under the expansive freedom of the sky, that all may see and hear."

Commanding both the Caer and the Port, it is probable that the summit of the Penton was crowned by a stone circle, probably oriented to the May sunrise, the new year of the Ancients, like so many of the existing Cornish circles. We owe to Sir Norman Lockyer the knowledge that the majority of circles were thus oriented. A very perfect example of one of these Gorsedds may be seen at Boscawen-Un, not far from the Land's End. Near the centre of the nineteen standing stones is a monolith, 8 feet out of the ground, which inclines to the north-east; one of the stones is a block of quartz 4 feet high, "obviously placed in a post of honour." "As a matter of fact, from it the May sun was seen to rise over the Index stone in the centre of the Circle." This remarkable circle is referred to in a Welsh Triad: "the Three Conventions of perfect song of the Isle of Britain: the Convention of Beiscawen in Dyvnwal, the Convention of Caer Caradwg in Lloegria, and the Convention of Brynn Gwyddon in Cymry" (Wales). It is suggested that Dyvnwal is the kingdom of Damnonium, and that Beiscawen is Boscawen Un. Caer Caradwg is the Hill of Caractacus in Salop; and Brynn Gwyddon is in Anglesea. That the circle of Boscawen Un was the centre of a large population in Druidic times is certain, from the numerous remains of British dwellings in the immediate neighbourhood. Many of the domed-stone roofs were in perfect condition until a few years ago, when one by one they were wantonly destroyed by idle youths on Sunday afternoons we were told by the farmer. And that this district, in the extreme West of Cornwall, was one of the headquarters of Druidical worship is shown by the remains of what appear to have been some of the finest and most elaborately constructed circles in the country, judging from Sir Norman Lockyer's account of Botallack, now completely destroyed by the erection on the site of the offices, etc., of the famous copper mine. At Boscawen, probably the Bards would assemble from all parts of the country for a convention of perfect song or Eisteddfod.

But to return to the Penton. It is probable that this circle was the principal observatory of Caer Troia, from the fact that within a few yards of the present reservoir, which is built on the actual summit, there is a well of unknown antiquity under Sadlers Wells Theatre, lined with masonry of ancient date, throughout its entire depth similar to the prehistoric wells we have already mentioned on the Windsor Table Mound, on the Wallingford Mound, and the well used by the first Astronomer Royal at Greenwich. Our present knowledge does not enable us to do more than call the reader's attention to the existence of these "telescope wells" (as they have been called) either pierced in the side of the Gorsedd, or, as in the case of the Bryn Gwyn and the Oxford Mounds, the well is now at the base of what may have been originally a shaft or funnel-shaped opening. The famous Holy Well in Dean's Yard, Westminster (referred to by Dean Stanley), may very possibly, nay probably was a Druidic well connected with the astronomical observations of the circle on Thorney and the Tothill.

That wells were used by the ancient astronomers we learn from Strabo, the Greek geographer. Describing his travels in Egypt, he says:

"At Syene is a well which indicates the summer solstice, because these places lie under the tropical circle, for on proceeding from the places in our country in Greece, I mean, the sun is there first overhead, and occasions the gnomons to be vertical shadows at noon, when the sun is vertical to us, it must necessarily cast its rays down wells, however deep they may be, to the water; for we, ourselves, stand in a perpendicular posture, and wells are dug perpendicularly to the surface."[1]

Pliny and Arrian both mention this well, and Eratosthenes, a distinguished member of the science school of Alexandria (276 B.C. to 176) accepting the proof that Syrene was under the tropic of Cancer, made use of the fact in computing the circumference of the earth. [2] Modern astronomers have found this method of making daylight observation so reliable that at the Potsdam and Wilson observatories, similar wells to those used by the Ancients have been made, fixed with mirrors. The old saying, "Truth lies at the bottom of a well," may probably be traced to the use of these wells in Druidic times.

In the interior of the Penton is a cave known as Merlin's Cave, which so late as the eighteenth century, when Islington Spa was a fashionable health-resort, and royalty came to enjoy the prospect and partake of syllabubs, appears to have been a kind of show-place. An underground passage at the bottom of the hill led to the cave; the entrance to which, in the cellars of *Merlin's Cave Tavern*, has only recently been bricked up, the passage being considered no longer safe. Whatever may be the value of the tradition connecting this cave with the astronomer Druid of King Arthur's Court, it is not inherently improbable that he who was—

> "The most famous man of all those times,
> Merlin, who knew the range of all their arts,
> Had built the King his havens, ships and halls,
> Was also Bard, and knew the starry Heavens.
> The people called him Wizard"—

should have carried on his astronomical studies in the neighbourhood of this ancient well on the Penton. Merlin's Cave may have been subsequently used as a Session House, from the example of the cave at the base of the Gorsedd at Oxford.

Many a solar and lunar festival has probably been cele-

[1] 1. Strabo, Book XVII, c.i.
[2] Lewis, *Astronomy of the Ancient*, p. 198.

brated upon the summit of the Penton, in which British kings have played their part; the presence of the sovereign appears to have been usual on these occasions of national rejoicing. We gather from the traditions and "Usages" of the Druidic order, that after the sacrifices had been offered by the priests within the precincts of the Circle, the Gorsedd procession was formed, and preceded by "Bards and Trumpeters," and escorted by the Druids, the "Ministers of the Sanctuary," the Monarch in his chariot, accompanied by his "Aiders in Council," proceeded to the Llandin, the *Great Seat or throne of the Monarch*, where the Gorsedd was solemnized in all the dignity of its symbolic ritual on the "Hill of Conference," familiar to us as Parliament Hill.

The memory of the old road by which the procession wended its way to the "Place of Assembly," survives in the name of "Maiden Lane," a railway station not far from Penton, probably on the site of the ancient way, which, under various names (for example, Kings Road), has been traced running in a north-easterly direction towards Highgate. In this name we have an interesting link with the first wave of Aryan settlers, "Maiden" being a corruption of the Sanskrit and Arabic word *Maidan*, signifying, Professor Margoliouth informs us, *an open place of public meeting*, like the "Maidan" of Calcutta and the "Maidan" of Cairo. Nor is this the only example of a Maiden Lane in London. Running parallel with the Strand is a "Maiden Lane" that opens out nearly opposite to the National Portrait Gallery, which less than two centuries ago was, like Trafalgar Square, an open space in the country, famous for its springs bubbling up in the grass near by (hence the origin of the name of Spring Gardens). The Keltic title for this green spot was the Bryn Vryn (gently rising bosom), from time immemorial a recognized "place of assembly" (like many such another in and around London) where the "Right of the People" to "Free Speech" cannot legally be interfered with. The preliminary proceedings of the Gorsedd or Eisteddfod probably were conducted here, as they would be in the market-place of a country town to-day by the members of the Order assembling and according to their official rank marshalled in procession and by way of Whitehall (the White or

Holy Hill or Hall) proceeded to the Circle on Thorney and the "Place of National Assembly," the Tothill.

At Canterbury, we find another example of the name Whitehall in the road leading direct to the Gorsedd of the Dane John.

The ancient sites of the Maiden Lanes of London have been so completely obscured by buildings and streets that it is satisfactory to find the descriptive meaning of the name confirmed by comparative antiquity at Colchester, where Maidenburgh Lane leads direct from the upper part of the town to the meadows beside the Colne at the foot of the Gorsedd Mound, on which King Coel's castle stands. Remains of the Roman Forum have been recently discovered on this spot, the site of the prehistoric "Place of Assembly." Another example is "Maiden Castle," a magnificent prehistoric earthwork near Dorchester; the inner area of which is $1\frac{1}{4}$ miles around and the ramparts in places 60 feet high, the probable place of national assembly for all the tribes of the district.

Having dealt with the two national Gorsedds of the Llandin and the Penton we now turn to the better known royal Gorsedds of the Bryn Gwyn and Tothill on the foreshore of the Thames. We distinguish them as royal because of their age-long connexion with British kings. We hear first about the Bryn Gwyn, or White Mound, as the burial place of Brutus and Imogene in about 1100 B.C., according to the generally accepted chronology. The next event connected with royalty of which we have any record is the burial of Dunwal Molmutius on the White Mount by his own request.

Under the double aspect of a road-maker and a law-giver we must devote a few words to this important character. In the chronological records of Wales, Dunwal Molmutius is called "One of the Three Wise Kings of Britain, and he established national municipal government." Shakespeare refers to Molmutius as the great Lawgiver and first King: " . . . Molmutius made our laws: Who was the first of Britain which did put his brows within a golden crown and called himself a King . . ." (*Cymbeline*, Act III. Sc. 1). The fact of Molmutius being styled the first King of Britain is explained by Hollinshed, who informs us that his predecessors were called

"Chiefs" and "Rulers," and these dignitaries, Harding states, wore only diadems.

> "The first he was, as Chroniclers exprime,
> That in this isle of Brittaine had crowne of golde,
> For all afore coper and gilte was to beholde."

Molmutius' name and fame is more especially associated with the traditions of Winton (Winchester), the southern capital where his merits have been publicly recognized. As a roadmaker we have his work in the seven converging roads like the spokes of a wheel in the old White City; three of these roads centred in London. For that Londinium was only second in importance is exemplified by Winton and London being the only places shown on an Anglo-Saxon map of the world preserved among the muniments of Hereford Cathedral. The Sarn Wyddelin was the high road from Dover to Holyhead, and Wyddelin or Gyddelin being the British term for Irish, the corruption into Watling Street is not great. The Sarn Ikin (Ickneild Street) led from Londinium northwards, through the Eastern districts and Sarn Achmaen, from Londinium to Menevia (St. David's). Sarn Achmaen, as it led to St. David's, probably derives its name, meaning a "rocking stone," from the great stone of Ceti in Gower, mentioned in the Triads as one of the "three mighty achievements of the island of Britain."

But it is as a lawgiver that Molmutius is best known. We have it on the authority of the great legal writers, Fortescue and Coke,[1] that the Molmutine Laws have been always regarded as the foundation and bulwark of British liberties, and have remained from his time the common, unwritten or native laws of the Island, as distinguished from the Roman, the canon and other codes of foreign introduction. A glance at the selection we append will show how many of these still remain in force. The Druidic Civil Laws, now for the first time systematized and reduced to a written code, are eminently distinguished for their clearness, brevity, justice and humanity. One of their strongest recommendations is that they are so

---

[1] *De Laudibus Legum Angliœ;* Coke, Preface to third volume of Pleadings; Origin of the Common Law of England.

simple as to be intelligible to all degrees of men and minds. King Alfred, it is recorded, employed his scribe Asser, a learned Welsh monk from Menevia (St. David's) (whom he afterwards made Abbot of Amesbury and Bishop of Sherborne), to translate the Molmutine Laws from the Keltic tongue into Latin, in order that he might incorporate them into his own Anglo-Saxon Code.

"There are three tests of Civil Liberty: equality of rights—equality of taxation—freedom to come and go.

'There are three causes which ruin a State: inordinate privileges—corruption of justice—national apathy.

"There are three things which cannot be considered solid longer than their foundations are solid: peace, property, and law.

"Three things are indispensable to a true union of nations: sameness of laws, rights and language.

"There are three things free to all Britons,—the forest, the unworked mine, the right of hunting wild creatures.

"There are three things that require the unanimous vote of the nation to effect: deposition of the sovereign—introduction of novelties in religion—suspension of law.

"There are three civil birthrights of every Briton: the right to go wherever he pleases—the right, wherever he is, to protection from his land and sovereign—the right of equal privileges and equal restrictions.

"There are three property birthrights of every Briton: five (British) acres of land for a home—the right of armorial bearings, the right of suffrage in the enacting of the laws, the male at twenty-one, the female on her marriage.

"There are three guarantees of society: security for life and limb—security for property—security of the rights of nature.

"There are three things the safety of which depends on that of the others: the sovereignty—national courage—just administration of the laws.

"There are three things which every Briton may legally be compelled to attend: the worship of God—military service—and the courts of law.

"There are three things free to every man, Briton or foreigner, the refusal of which no law will justify: water from spring, river, or well—firing from a decayed tree—a block of stone not in use.

"There are three orders who are exempt from bearing arms:

the bard—the judge—the graduate in law or religion. These represent God and His peace, and no weapon must ever be found in their hand.

"There are three whose power is kingly in law: the sovereign paramount of Britain over all Britain and its isles—the princes palatine in their princedoms— the heads of the clans in their clans.

"There are three sacred things by which the conscience binds itself to truth: the name of God—the rod of him who offers up prayers to God—the joined right hand.

"There are three persons who have a right to public maintenance: the old—the babe—the foreigner who cannot speak the British tongue."

These laws of Molmutius are briefly summarized by Spenser:

> "Then made he lawes; which some men say
> Were unto him revealed in vision,
> By which he freed the Traveller's highway,
> The Churches' part, the Ploughman's portion;
> Restraining stealth, and strong extortion,
> The gracious Numa of great Britanny,
> For till his dayes, the chief dominion
> By strength was wielded without policy.
> Therefore he first wore crown of gold for dignity."

After a memorable reign of forty years Molmutius died, and was interred on the White Mound in Caer Troia. His eldest son, Belinus, succeeded him, and completed the roads his father began. A law was made throwing open these roads to all nations and foreigners, and placing them on the same footing of security as the river and the sanctuaries. "There are three things free to a country and its borders—the rivers, the roads, and the place of worship. These are under the protection of God and His peace. Whoever on or within them draws weapons against any one is a criminal." In this law originated the term "the King's Highway."

Within the precincts of the Bryn Gwyn, Belinus erected a royal residence or castle with "many towers, one of wondrous height." He caused a stupendous embankment on the Thames to be constructed, and a quay for the ships of the

"Porth." Belinus died at the age of eighty. His body was burnt, and the ashes deposited in a golden urn on the top of the highest tower of his palace. The tradition survives in the familiar name of "Billingsgate," "Belin's Gate."

In the Welsh Mabinogion, "Bendigeid Vran, the son of Llyr," is referred to as "a crowned king of this island, exalted from the crown of London." Wounded in the foot by a poisoned arrow fighting against the Irish, Bendigeid commanded his followers to cut off his head and bear it even unto the White Mount in London and bury it there with its face towards France. . . ." "And they buried the head in the White *Mount,* and when it was buried this was the third Goodly concealment; and it was the third ill-fated disclosure when it was disinterred, inasmuch as no invasion from across the sea came to this island while the head was in that concealment." The name of this king is not mentioned in the genealogies, but he may possibly appear under another title.

Belin Mawr in 100 B.C., the descendant and successor of Belin I, is the next British king whose name we find associated with the traditions of the Bryn Gwyn. Belin Mawr is said to have resided here, presumably in the castle of "many towers," built by his ancestor within the precincts of the royal demesne. No single instance can be found of a Keltic king erecting any kind of building upon the site of a sacred mound. At Windsor, Caerleon, and Old Sarum, the castle, and royal residences stand round about the foot of the Mound. At Camulodunum the remains of King Coel's Castle are to be seen at Lexden, now a suburb of Colchester, a mile or so from the grand old Gorsedd upon which the Emperor Claudius erected the present (so-called) King Coel's Castle as a sign of "Eternal Dominion." It was the seizure of the Druidical emoluments for the worship of the gods and the deified Claudius upon this sacred mound, according to Tacitus, that led to the national rising under Boadicea. The only time London has been rifled and destroyed has not been by a foreign enemy but by a British queen and a British army visiting it with condign punishment for its collusion with a foreign invader.

It is generally thought the Britons of this period were savages, clothed in skins. Quite the contrary was the case, as we learn from Strabo, a contemporary of King Cunobeline, who has left us a most vivid description of the dress of the Britons at this period, which removes the false impression that the inhabitants of our island were a race of semi-civilized barbarians as regards their personal appearance and weapons. The Greek geographer writes:

"He came, not clad in skins like a Scythian, but with a bow in his hand, a quiver hanging on his shoulders, a plaid wrapped about his body, a gilded belt encircling his loins, and trousers reaching from the waist down to the soles of his feet. He was easy in his address; agreeable in his conversation; active in his despatch, and secret in his management of great affairs; quick in judging of present accuracies; and ready to take his part in any sudden emergency: provident withal in guarding against futurity: diligent in the quest of wisdom: fond of friendship: trusting very little to fortune, yet having the entire confidence of others, and trusted with everything for his prudence. He spoke Greek with a fluency, that you would have thought he had been bred up in the Lyceum, and conversed all his life with the Academy of Athens."

Heli or Beli II reigned forty years and had three sons, Llud, Caswallon (Cassivellaunus) and Nennius. Lludd succeeded him. From the testimony of many old writers, whose accounts of him all tally in a most remarkable way, Lludd appears to have inherited a love of building from his ancestor, Belin I, and a similar desire to hand down his name to posterity as a benefactor of Caer Troia. He is best known as the founder of Ludgate, the western gate of the city (66 B.C.), and was buried in a vault under this gate. Holinshed states:

"Lludd began to reign in 72 B.C., seventeen years before the Romans came. He made a strong wall of lime and stone and fortified it with divers fair towers, and in the west part of the same wall he erected a strong gate, which he commanded to be called after his name 'Ludgate,' and so unto this day, it is called Ludgate. . . . He caused buildings to be made between London stone and Ludgate and builded for himself not far from the said gate a fair palace which is the Bishop of London's palace, beside Paules at this day as some think; yet Harrison supposes it to have been Baynard's Castle, where the Black Friars now standeth."

122

Lludd's attempt to beautify the city is thus described in the ancient Welsh MSS. of the Mabinogion preserved in Jesus College, Oxford, translated by Lady Charlotte Guest.

"Lludd ruled prosperously and rebuilt the walls of London and encompassed it about with numberless towers. After that he bade the citizens build houses therein, such as no houses in the kingdom could equal. Moreover he was a mighty warrior and generous and liberal in giving meat and drink to all who sought them, and though he had many castles and cities, this one loved he more than any. And he dwelt therein most part of the year and therefore it was called Caer Lludd and afterwards Caer London."

From the same source we learn that Lludd caused the Isle of Britain to be measured in its length and in its breadth, and in Oxford he found the central point. This is confirmed by Mr. Stanford, the great authority on all topographical matters at the present time. That Oxford was an important centre in early British times is proved by the existence, as we have seen, of a fine prehistoric, artificial circular mound, within the precincts of the ancient royal castle.

It is further recorded that Lludd issued an edict commanding the city to be henceforth called Llud-din instead of Caer Troia. Gildas, the British historian, writing in the sixth century, mentions that the people, headed by Nennius, threatened to rise and depose Lludd if the edict was carried out. He was compelled to give way. This contention seems to suggest that the old herioc name of Troynovant, bestowed by Brutus on the Porth of the Tain, had never completely superseded the yet older and more popular Kymric title of the Llan-din, from remote antiquity the "seat" of government in the great capital of commerce. If the mounds had not been already there, the resemblance to the historic Troy would not have impressed Brutus. As the sacred name of the Winton survives to this day the official title of the southern capital, in like manner (we venture to think) do the traditions of the Llandin survive in the titles of the Bishop and the Diocese, the Mayor and Corporation of the city of London.

Lludd's two sons were too young to rule, so that by the

"voice of the people" Cassivellaunus was crowned king and made military dictator under the title of Pendragon. The city of Trinovantum, with the Duchy of Kent, was given to Androgeus, the Duchy of Cornwall to Tenuantius. In 55 B.C. Cæsar landed in Britain. With four thousand chariots Cassivellaunus opposed him. Nennius attacked the 10th Legion. Cæsar was assailed by Nennius in person. The sword of the great Roman buried itself in the shield of the British prince, and before he could extricate it, the tide of battle separated the combatants, leaving the weapon a trophy to be long afterwards exhibited to the inhabitants of Caer Troia.[1] Nennius died from the effect of the wound inflicted by the famous "Mors Crocea" and was buried in the Bryn Gwyn.

Androgeus, or Avarwy, Lludd's elder son, had made a secret treaty, undertaking to open the gates of London to Cæsar. The plot, however, was unsuccessful. This act of treachery procured for him among the mass of the people the opprobrious name of "Mandubrad," the Black Traitor, perpetuated, in Cæsar's *Commentaries*, in the form of Manubratius. This man was consigned to eternal infamy in the Triads of his country as the first of the "three capital traitors of the island of Britain." Avarwy and many of his partisans took refuge from the storm of national execration on board the Roman fleet and returned to Rome with Cæsar after his fifty-five days' campaign. The Black Traitor, Avarwy, died prior to the assassination of Cæsar in Rome.

In the following lines Spenser gives us the history of the events of the next few years:

"He left two sons, too young to rule aright,
Ahdrorogeus and Tenantius, pictures of his might."

"Whilst they were young, Cassibalane their eme (uncle)
Was by the people chosen in their sted,
Who on him tooke the royall diademe,
And goodly well long time it governed;

---

[1] According to tradition, Constantine the Great carried away this famous sword of the "yellow death" to Constantinople, but we have been unable to trace it.

Till the prowd Romans him disquieted,
And warlike Caesar, tempted with the name
Of this sweet island, never conquered,
And envying the Briton's blazed fame.
(O hideous hunger of dominion) hither came.

"Yet twise they were repulsed backe againe,
And twise renforst back to their ships did fly
The whilst with blood they all the Shore did staine,
And the gray ocean into purple dy:

Ne had they footing found at last perdie,
Had not Androgeus, false to native soyle,
And envious of uncles soveraintie,
Betrayd his countrey unto forreine spoyle,
Nought els but treason from the first this land did foyle.

"So by him Cæsar got the victory,
Through great bloudshed, and many a sad assay,
In which him selfe was charged heavily
Of hardy Nennius, whom he yet did slay,
But lost his sword, yet to be seene this day.
Thenceforth this land was tributarie made
T'ambitious Rome, and did their rule obey,
Till Arthur all that reckoning defrayd;
Yet oft the Briton kings against them strongly swayd.

"Next him Tenantius reigned. . . ."

(*Faerie Queene*, Book II, canto x.)

In the reign of King John we hear of Lludd's Gate, when in 1215 the Barons came to London to compel the King to sign the Magna Charta. While waiting for the King's consent, riots broke out. They stormed the Jews' Quarter in the neighbourhood of Ludgate and used the materials thus obtained in repairing the damage done to the wall and gate. Evidence of the fact was found some years later, when stones, inscribed with Hebrew characters, were found embedded in the masonry of the gate. In 1260, during the reign of Henry III, the gate was again repaired and adorned with figures of Lludd and his two sons, Androgeus and Tenuantius. During

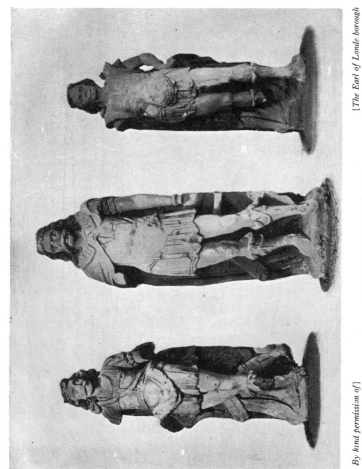

KING LLUDD AND HIS SONS

(From old Temple Bar, now in the grounds of St. Dunstan's, Regent's Park)

the reign of Edward VI, the populace, in their hatred of all images, knocked off the heads of Lludd and his sons—these were restored by Mary; but during the reign of Elizabeth the gate was entirely taken down and rebuilt, new figures of Lludd and his sons being put on the eastern side. Thus the gate stood till 1760, when it was finally taken down and the statues granted to Sir Francis Gosselin. The late Marquis of Hertford eventually purchased them with St. Dunstan's clock. These and the clock he erected in Hertford Villa, Regent's Park, now called St. Dunstan's. Lord Londesborough, the present owner, kindly gave the writer permission for photographs to be taken of these historical representations of King Lludd and his sons.

According to the Welsh chronicles and a tradition recorded by Morgan in his Cambrian History, Cassivellaunus, after peace had been concluded at Verulam, chivalrously entertained Cæsar at the White Tower for seven days, while the embarkation of the Roman army was proceeded with in Kent. Colour is lent to this tradition by the fact that one of the towers of the oldest part of the fortifications, the "Salt Tower," is known to this day as Cæsar's Tower. "Salt," a corruption of Sol (like the Eton montem example of "Salt Hill"), is a name which takes us back to early British times, and suggests that this ancient structure may have been originally the "Clock" Tower of King Belin's Castle. When the records of the Tower of London come to be published we may learn if the tradition of Cæsar's sojourn within its walls has any foundation in fact; and some clue may be found as to the origin of Roman masonry that still may be seen in different parts of the old buildings that on two sides encircle William the Norman's White Tower.

The Bryn Gwyn in Cæsar's time, we should remember, was still in its original condition, simply a green conical mound, with no building whatever upon it, consecrated to the service of the Most High, and venerated as the burial-place of two of the most illustrious of our prehistoric British kings, Brutus, the reputed founder of London, and Molmutius, the "Solon" of Britain, of whom Keltic lore records he was a "restorer and protector of the ancient sanctuaries, and of the high-ways that led to them," showing that the religious monuments of Britain were regarded as old even in his time, *circa* 500 B.C.

Shortly before Cæsar's stay at the Tower, Nennius, the British prince, died here in the palace of his forefathers, after a lingering illness of three weeks, from the effects of a wound he had received from Cæsar's sword (the *morscrocea*), and had been laid to rest in the bosom of the Holy Hill; an interesting tradition that links the British Gorsedd with historical times.

It is with the continuity of the prehistoric traditions of the Bryn Gwyn that we must now deal; these are certainly worthy of consideration, slender as may be the connexion between the Kymric customs and those that still survive, in one or two instances, to the present time. That the White Mount was the seat of a prehistoric observatory is probable from the existence in the basement of a well 150 feet deep, lined with stone throughout like that of the Penton; it is only recently that this ancient well has been enclosed with iron railing; it is now said by the authorities to be a Roman well. The north-east turret of the present Norman structure has from time immemorial been used as an observatory, and only ceased to be used as such when Charles II removed the Royal Observatory to his royal demesne in Greenwich Park. Tower Hill as a place of National Assembly, like Parliament Hill, carries on to this day its traditions. Seldom a dinner hour passes without a crowd assembling to listen to some popular demagogue. A few years since a band of Macedonian gipsies settled down upon Tower Hill with their caravans, secure in their traditional knowledge that it was common ground; and special legal measures had to be adopted before they could be removed. Surely in this unprecedented action of these poor foreigners may be traced the imperishable traditions of an ancient kinship.

Is it a mere coincidence, we wonder, that the summit of the British Gorsedd should retain its sanctity as a consecrated place of worship to this day, crowned as it is by the Conqueror's Norman chapel, dedicated to the Midsummer Saint John Baptist? Here William of Normandy and his Queen are said to have knelt in prayer, and there for well-nigh a thousand years Divine Service has been celebrated within the walls of this chapel. Immediately under the roof, from the time of Henry Beauclerc to Charles II, it was the ancient custom of the kings of England to assemble before proceeding to Westminster to be crowned. On the even of their coronation, the ministers and nobles met in council to nominate the sovereign. The following morning all assembled in the chapel on the topmost storey of the building, and there the procession was formed which conducted the king in state through the city to the royal seat at Westminster, where within the Abbey, the ancient site of the Druidical circle, the anointing and crowning took place. May not this be a survival of the Kymric custom practised on Silbury Hill and Abury, where after that by the "voice of the people" the king had been elected and lifted by the "elders in council" to a stone seat or chair, the religious ceremonial of anointing took place within the precincts of the Circle?

From Roman to Norman times, with but one exception in the sixth century, we can find no mention whatever, either in history or tradition, of the White Mound. But that it was a royal stronghold in King Arthur's time, we gather from Book XXI of Sir Thomas Malory's *Morte d'Arthur*, in which he relates—

"How Sir Mordred presumed and took on him to be King of England, and would have married the Queen, his Uncle's wife. Wherefore Sir Mordred made a parliament, and called the lords together, and there he made them to choose him King; and so was he crowned at Canterbury, and held a feast there, fifteen days; and afterwards he drew him into Winchester, and there he took the Queen Guenever, and said plænly that he would wed her which was his uncle's wife. And so he made ready for the feast and a day prefixed that they should be wedded; wherefore Queen Guenever was passing heavy. But she durst not discover her heart, but spake faer, and agreed to Sir Mordred's will. Then she desired of Sir Mordred for to go to London, to buy all manner of things that longed unto the wedding. Any by cause of her faer speech Sir Mordred trusted her well enough and gave her leave to go. And so when she came to London she took the Tower of London, and suddenly in all haste possible she stuffed it with all manner of victual, and well garnished it with men, and so kept it. Then when Sir Mordred wist and understood how he was beguiled, he was passing wroth out of measure. And a short tale to make, he went and laid a mighty siege about the Tower of London, and made many great assults thereat, and threw many great engines unto them, and shot great guns. But all might not prevail Sir Mordred, for Queen Guenever would never, for faer speech nor for foul, trust to come on his hands again. . . . Then Sir Mordred sought on Queen Guenever by letters and sondes, and by daer means and foul means, for to have her to come out of the Tower of London; but all this availed not, for she answered him shortly, openly and privily, that she had lever slay herself than to be married with him. Then came word to Sir Mordred that King Arthur had araised the siege for Sir Lancelot, and he was coming homeward with a great host to be avenged on Sir Mordred. . . ."

The above account of Queen Guenever taking refuge in the Tower of London, we may be sure, was no flight of Sir Thomas Malory's fancy, but was founded on fact. For Margaret of Richmond, the most learned lady of the day, and the patroness also of learning at the Universities of Oxford and Cambridge, had specially employed the old Welsh knight, at her own cost, to collect, sift and garner material for writing the *Morte d'Arthur* from Welsh MSS. then extant, traditions and legends in Wales and Cornwall, and historical data, wherever he could find it concerning the British King Arthur, "the first of the most Christian worthies of the world" (see Caxton's preface to the *Morte d'Arthur*), from whom her son Henry Tudor, the heir-presumptive to the throne, was lineally descended. As directress of the education of the young princesses, this astute lady was residing at the time at the Court of Edward IV at Westminster, and we find indications that she took a personal interest in the printing of the *Morte d'Arthur* in the Almonry of the Abbey. The one object Lady Margaret had in view was the future advancement of her son, and in no better way could this be done, she conceived, than by kindling an interest in the fascinating and romantic history of the Keltic King among the chivalry and nobility of the Court—men who would have it in their power, if ever the opportunity offered, of supporting her son's claims to the throne of his forefathers. No book ever achieved its purpose better or contributed more to make a cause popular. Malory's zeal and his love of "King Arthur and his noble Knights of the Round Table" was infectious, and stirred both the imagination and the hearts of all who read in his beautiful English prose (valued to this day for its style) the character sketches of the "goodly fellowship" men whose ardour in redressing human wrongs has set the standard for all time of British manhood. So that when in the mysterious dispensation of Providence a few years later the time came that the Keltic monarchy was once again restored in the person of this illustrious lady's son Henry VII, the imperishable ideals of the Round Table lent a peculiar and special glamour to the prophesied return from his long exile in Brittany of the representative of the ancient line of British kings, the "Dragon of the great Pendragonship" of Wales.

We now turn to the consideration of the royal Gorsedd beside the ford and ferry in the West—namely, the Tothill, Westminster. This has retained much longer than the Bryn Gwyn its royal associations. Pre-eminently the "Great Seat" of Royalty in London here from time immemorial British kings have held their courts and their councils. An old map in the British Museum shows the site of the prehistoric Tot, or sacred Pile on Tothill fields, of which no trace remains, though its memory survives to this day in the names of the old tournament ground and in Tothill Street.

The ancient royal palace is reputed to have been a magnificent and extensive pile fronting the river, in part covering the ground now occupied by the two large areas or courts known as Old Palace Yard and New Palace Yard. It consisted of a great number of buildings destined to various purposes. On the site of the original Great Hall of the British King's palace William Rufus built the present Hall, and the site of the crypt under the Chapel of St. Stephen's, tradition says, was originally the Oratory of Edward the Confessor. Westminster was the favourite residence of this saintly monarch. It was not until the ancient palace had been almost wholly destroyed by fire that Henry VIII bought Whitehall from Cardinal Wolsey

—a purchase which put an end to most of the royal glories of Westminster. But as the seat of the High Court of Parliament, and of our legal tribunal the traditions of Druidic and British legislation have survived in unbroken continuity.

The earliest historical account that has reached us of the Gorsedd Mound of the Tot-hill and the circle on Thorney is in connexion with the British King Lleuver Mawr in the second century A.D. On the site of the Druidic circle Lucius, the Latinized name of the British king, erected a church; and the Druidic College in connexion with the services of the Gorsedd he is said to have converted to the use of the Christian clergy. The existence of the Druidical College may have given rise to the title of Westminster Abbey as the "Collegiate Church." Dean Buckland held that the Druidical College stood on the site of the present College Gardens. It may have been on account of this organized community of Druids and Bards that King Lucius not only built a church, but "by his free grant, ordained freedom of sanctuary as a means to allure his people to the true worship of God," assured that his subjects would be well looked after and kept from doing further harm by those wise and learned administrators of law and order.

The privileges of this ancient Sanctuary one thousand years later were renewed by Edward the Confessor, in a charter in which it is recapitulated that Lucius had previously established a sanctuary by royal charter. Notwithstanding its royal patrons, it was swept away at the time of the Reformation, and only the memory of the site survives in the name of the sanctuary in the Broadway, Westminster.

We find in a note in Stanley's *Memorials of Westminster*, a pathetic account of how Fackenham, the last of the Abbots, convinced of the righteousness of his cause, armed with a royal charter under each arm and accompanied only by one monk, in February 1555, pleaded in the House of Commons for the retention of the Sanctuary about to be abolished by Henry VIII. In his eloquent address we have documentary proof that Lucius was the founder of the first Church at Westminster.

"And first, for the antiquity of Sanctuary at Westminster. It may please you to have consideration how it is no less than 1,400 years since Sanctuary was there first ordained: for Lucius, the first Christian King of this realm who, about 100 years after Christ, received the Christian faith from the holy Pope of Rome and martyr Eleutherius, by the ministry of the holy monk Fagan (whom some call Fagan and Damian), immediately after that he was by the said holy monk baptized, and instructed in the true profession of Christ's religion, did destroy the Temple that then stood here at Westminster dedicated to the idol Apollo, and in place thereof erected a new Temple to the honour of the True God, our Saviour Jesus Christ, and of St. Peter, from whose sanctity he received the benefits of Christianity: and there he, by his free grants, ordained Sanctuary. . . . He, I say, made proclamation that whoever would resort thither, and worship the True God and embrace the true faith (which he had then received) should enjoy free pardon and immunity from all offences by them committed. . . . The Cursed Danes that over-ran this realm, as we read in histories, they destroyed faith and Sanctuary: and so stood it dissolved till the time of the holy King St. Edward. He restored faith and Sanctuary: he revived again the freedom and privilege there, and not only revived the same, but confirmed them also with his most ample charter. . . ."

To this day, the open space fronting the West Doors of the Abbey is known as "Broad Sanctuary," a name which perpetuates the memory of the place of refuge established by Lleuver Mawr, "the Great Light," nearly 2,000 years ago, under the shadow of the Tot-hill.

A contempoary life of Edward the Confessor in the Harleian MSS. throws an interesting light upon this British settlement in the marshes in the eleventh century.

"The devout King destined to God that place both for that it was near unto the famous and wealthy city of London, and also had a pleasant situation amongst fruitful fields lying round about it, with the principal river running hard by, bringing in from all parts of the world great variety of wares and merchandise of all sorts to the city adjoining: but chiefly for the love of the Chief Apostle whom he reverenced with a special and singular affection."

From the sixth to the sixteenth century we find constant

reference made to numerous jousts held on the royal tilting ground. But of none have we so full an account as of the "great jousts and tourneys" ordained by King Arthur. [1] Malory gives full details of several of these, to mention but one summons.

"And the cry was made that the day of the jousts should be beside Westminster upon Candlemas Day, whereof many Knights were glad and made them ready to be at these jousts in the freshest manner. In Book XIX we have a charming description of 'How Queen Guenever rode on Maying with certain Knights of the Round Table and clad all in Green.'

"So it befell in the month of May, Queen Guenever called unto her Knights of the Table Round; and she gave them warning that early upon the morrow she would ride on Maying into the woods and fields beside Westminster. And I warn you that there be none of you but that he be well horsed and that ye all be clothed in green, either in silk, outher in cloth, and I shall bring with me ten ladies, and every Knight shall have a lady behind him, and every Knight shall have a squire and two yeomen; and I will they be all well horsed." . . . "And so upon the morn they took their horses with the Queen and rode on Maying in woods and meadows as it pleased them, in great joy and delights." . . . "So as the Queen had Mayed and all her Knights, and all were be dashed with herbs, mosses and flowers in the best manner and freshest—right so came out of the wood Sir Meliagrance with an eight score men——"

We refer our reader to the text of the *Morte d'Arthur*, if curious to learn the end of this Maying expedition which started so happily.

Throughout the Middle Ages Tothill Fields retained its popularity as a royal tilting-ground. Nor did it diminish under the Tudor kings. For here was held the famous tournament in honour of the marriage of Henry VII to Elizabeth of York, who, like her husband, had Keltic royal blood in her veins, a fact that is brought prominently into notice in the design of the brass closure of the royal tomb of Henry Tudor and his Queen in Westminster Abbey. Here Henry VIII established his Society of Archers, the beginning of the Royal

[1] In the King's Robing Room of the Palace of Westminster, the history of King Arthur is set forth in carved panels from birth to death, while Dyce's magnificent pictures, illustrating the virtues of chivalry, adorn the walls.

Artillery Company incorporated by Royal Charter in 1537. And several magnificent tournaments were held here in Queen Elizabeth's time, when the old Tothill was still standing.

Before we bring these fragmentary notes on the prehistoric mounds and circles of London to a conclusion, as we are about to do, with a description of an actual modern Gorsedd, solemnized as in pre-Christian times, within a stone circle on "some green spot, in the face of the sun, the eye of Light," with all the ancient symbolic ceremonial laid down by the Founder, it is important to glance at the historical evidence that has reached us of the functions of a Gorsedd, the "oldest educational institution in Europe" (according to Matthew Arnold), an Institution, moreover, not known out of Britain.

Established in 1000 B.C. by Aedd Mawr and the three Wisemen he selected to assist him in the organization of the Druidic Order, the laws and regulations of the "Gorsedd of the Isle of Britain" were handed down by oral traditions for the first five centuries after creation by Bards specially set apart to rehearse these laws in the audience of the people at the annual assembly of the Gorsedd or Eisteddfod. From *Barddas* (being a collection of original documents illustrative of the Theology, Wisdom and Usages of the Bardo-Druidic system published by the Welsh MSS. Society in 1852), we now learn that the Druidic Gorsedd Laws were incorporated by the British King Dunwal Molmutius, who lived in the fifth century B.C., in his famous code; and it is from this reliable source that we find the "Gorsedd of the Bards" is mentioned as "the oldest in its origin" of the "three privileged Gorsedds of the Isle of Britain." And that there were three Gorsedds according to the privilege of the country and nation of the Kymry, having their respective duties for the improvement of society.

"The first is the Gorsedd of the Bards of the Isle of Britain and their foundation and privilege rest upon reason, nature, and cogency; or according to other teachers and wise men, upon reason, Nature and circumstance. And the privilege and office of those protected by the Gorsedd of Bards are to maintain and preserve and diffuse authorized instruction in the sciences of piety, wisdom, and courtesy; and to preserve memorial and record of everything commendable respecting individuals and kindred; and every event of times; and every natural phenomenon; and wars; and regulations and country and nation; and punishments and commendable victories; and to preserve a warranted record of genealogies, marriages, nobility, privileges, and customs of the nation of the Kymry; and to attend the exigencies of other Gorsedds on announcing what shall be achieved, and what shall be requisite, and under lawful proclamation and warning; and further than this there is nothing either of office or of privilege attached to a Gorsedd of Bards.

"Second the Gorsedd of the country and commonwealth; or the Gorsedd of judicature and decision of law, for the right and protection of the country and nation, their refugees and aliens. These Gorsedds act severally; that is to say, the Gorsedd of federate support makes a law where an occasion requires, and confirms it in a country; and that is not allowed to a country distinct from a federate country. The Gorsedd of judgment and judicature decides upon such as shall transgress the law, and punishes him. And the Gorsedd of the Bards teaches commendable sciences, and decides respecting them, and methodically preserves all the memorials of the nation to insure their authenticity. And it is not right for any one of these Gorsedds to intermeddle with the deliberation of either of the other two, but to confirm them, and to support them regularly.

"The third Gorsedd, or that of federate support in its original and determinate purpose, is to effect what may be necessary as to anything new, and as to the improvement of the laws of a country and federate country by a federate jury of chiefs of kindreds, wise men, and sovereign ruler. A sovereign prince, or ruler of paramount right, is the oldest in possessive title of the kings and the princes of a federate community: and he is to raise the mighty agitation of the country."

According to the tenor of this extract it was "the Gorsedd of judgment and judicature" that possessed the special right of determining national and social disputes, in conformity with the law that was enacted in a "Gorsedd of federate support." They were matters of a literary character mainly that came under the supervision of the Bards: nevertheless, there was some connexion between the three institutions. They were "to confirm, and support" each other "regularly." The Bards were required more particularly to register the events that occurred in country and nation, to preserve the records of genealogies, marriages, nobility, privileges and customs, of the nation of the Kymry. There seems therefore no reason to dismiss as untrustworthy, and, as we have been so repeatedly told, "not worth the parchment they are written on," the genealogies of the British kings and the historical events recorded in the Welsh "Bruts," events which furthermore we find, for the most part, imperishably crystallized in the traditions of the localities where they occurred.

Having satisfied ourselves from original sources preserved in the original Kymric tongue, the "oldest living language in Europe," of the value of the Gorsedd institution as an organized "governing body," we must see what Sir Norman Lockyer and other scientists of our own time have discovered with regard to the scientific construction of these prehistoric open-air Sanctuaries which prove conclusively that these Circles were used by the ancients not only as places of worship, dedicated to the service of the Most High and as Courts of Justice, but were also Observatories. The Rev. J. Griffith in an article in *Nature* (May 2, 1907) has been the first to set forth the scientific significance of a Welsh Gorsedd circle and to explain the meaning of the three stones pointing outwards that one sees lying on the ground at the entrance to a Gorsedd circle to-day. He states that "the present Gorsedd circle consists of twelve stones, 30° apart, with a larger stone in the centre. Outside, on the East, three stones are placed to indicate the solstices and equinoxes to an observer at the central stone"; and he quotes the following nomenclature of the stones: "The stones forming the circle are called the *White Stones*, or *Stone of Testimony*; the circle itself is sometimes called the *White Circle*." The middle stone, or altar, is termed *Maen Gorsedd*, i.e. Presidential Stone.

"The stones pointing to the Equinoxes and Solstices are called *Stones of the Sun*. The Bards stand unshod, uncovered, within the circle; the Presiding Bard, who must be of the *Primitive Order*, stands by the *Presidial Stone*. All the other Bards attend around, standing near the *White Stones* or Periphery of the circle."

Mr. Griffith's researches enable him to prove that the Solstitial Stones have really replaced others so located that the sunrise places in May and November were indicated. In Gorsedd history, then, the May year came first and was indicated by the position of the stones.

The sign which Mr. A. L. Lewis (*Nature*, June 6, 1907) associates naturally with the "broad arrow" is really a "miniature May Gorsedd."

Even more than the ancient codes of Welsh laws, says Mr. Griffith, the Bardic traditions of the Gorsedd are the most formally authenticated of any Welsh literature. Since the tenth century [1] the former have had to take care of themselves apparently, but the Bardic traditions were always recited at every proper Gorsedd.

"From the twelfth century to the first quarter of the nineteenth we have accounts of a series of great Gorsedds (or Eisteddfods, the same thing) every one of which was convened for the chief purpose of re-codifying or otherwise dealing with the Bardic traditions. We have nothing so well and faithfully guarded in Welsh literature as our Bardic traditions."

"Mr. Griffith," says Sir Norman Lockyer, "has rendered another service to archæology in its widest sense by pointing out in a subsequent article the enormous number of Welsh and English fairs held on the festival (quarter) days of the May year. These, doubtless, are the modern representations of the assemblies at the festivals of places where circles existed, or where fires were lighted or Gorsedds erected; so that it may be said that fairs as well as many old churches mark for us the loci of the original circle worship, and the fact that we are dealing with the May Year and *not* the solstice shows that we have to do with a very high antiquity." "We are able to see," Mr. Griffith remarks, "at the Welsh National Eisteddfod in this twentieth century, the actual use to which the temple observatory was put. If such a broad assertion causes surprise it is considerably lessened by what seems to me to be an incontrovertible fact, that instead of having one

---

[1] In the tenth century A.D. Howel the Good of Dyfed constituted and gave laws to be kept through his dominions, which were used in Wales till such time as the inhabitants received the laws of England in the time of Edward I.

Gorsedd, and that in Wales, a true survival from late Neolithic times (to fix a downward limit), we have in Britain thousands of Gorsedds, the pedigrees of which are as unimpeachable as that of the Welsh institution. I refer to fairs still held on the quarter days of the May Year. To a student of the Welsh Gorsedd this at once dispels any *à priori* doubt as to the antiquity of that institution . . . the Gorsedd and the popular fair is one and the same, constituting a true monument as ancient as a temple observatory in stone. A better way of putting it is, the temple observatory has survived in (1) stone, in (2) tradition, and in (3) festival. The Welsh Gorsedd presents this three-ply evidence." (See Sir Norman Lockyer's *Stonehenge and Other British Stone Monuments Astronomically Considered.*)

Those of my readers who desire to recall a Druidic assembly on the site of St. Paul's, the Abbey, or within the precincts of any other of our British circles, cannot do better than be present at one of the National Gorsedds in Wales. The locality is chosen always at the Eisteddfod of the previous year—usually a meadow, just outside the town—large enough to afford standing room for the thousands of all sorts and conditions in life, and of all denominations who assemble to take part in these popular, purely educational contests, as they now are.

A circle is formed of 12 unhewn stones symbolic of the signs of the zodiac. In the centre is the large Maen Llog or Logan Stone, symbolic of the "Rock" which is Christ. Druidism itself was ordinarily known as "Y Maen," *the stone*. The Maen Llog must be placed in a central position and must be untouched by any tool. It is supposed to have the same symbolic significance as the sacred rock on Mount Moriah, that rises from the rocky platform of Mount Sion. The name Sion signifies stone, and Mount Sion, the Mount of the Stone, has been regarded from the time of David and Solomon as the most sacred ground in Jerusalem. The stone is still here on the original site. Before the Holy City came into the possession of the Mussulman, the Christians regarded this curious monument of old Jerusalem as the "Rock of the Holy of Holies, and it must have formed an essential feature of the Temple

Area," says Dean Stanley. The great unhewn mass of rock is believed to rest on one point of junction only, with the rocky platform of the Mount. Immense stress is laid by the Moham-medans on what they consider the miraculous suspension of the Stone above the Mount. There is little doubt but that the venerable relic on the Temple Area in the Holy City was at one time a rocking stone, rocking in imitation of the move-ment of the Sacred Ark, and on this account was regarded by the Ancients as the type of the Ark; hence the origin of the term "Logan Stone" as applied to the rocking stones of Great Britain, and the Maen Llogan of the Welsh Gorsedd Circle!

Twelve Bards, one by each stone, guard the Gorsedd Circle to-day as in times past, and two Keepers of the Gate are stationed at the entrance, which is on the East side. The ground plan of the Welsh Circle is similar to that of Stone-henge. At the entrance of the Circle may be seen three prostrate unhewn stones pointing outwards from the central "Maen Llogan"; these represent the ancient Kymric symbol of the Awen, or Holy Wings, the three rays or rods of light signifying the Eye of Light, or the radiating light of the Divine Intelligence shed upon the Druidic Circle.

In the Iolo MSS. (a selection from the ancient Welsh writings, published by the Welsh MSS. Society) the origin is given of this ancient hierogram, which analyses into the three bardic letters of the "ineffable name," "I AM," JH VH, JEHOVAH, answering to the Christian device of I.H.S., the emblem that has come down to us along the ages in the "Holy Wings," the "Logos" or the "Voice" of the Supreme God. On three occasions only in God's Word do we find the utterance of the Divine Name mentioned—at the burning bush, in our Lord's words, "Before Abraham was, I am," and in the Garden of Gethsemane, when Our Lord said to those who had come to take Him, "I AM HE," [1] and the men and officers "went backward and fell to the ground."

"The announcement of the Divine name is the first event traditionally preserved and it occurred as follows: 'God, in vouchsafing His Name, said /|\ and, with the Word, all worlds

[1] Exodus iii. 14. John viii. John xviii. 5.

and animations sprang co-instantaneously to being, and from their non-existence, shouting in ecstasy of joy /|\, and thus repeating the Name of the Deity. Still and small was that melodious sounding voice (that is the Divine Utterance) which will never be equalled again, until God shall renovate every pre-existence from the primary utterance of which emanated all lays and melodies, whether of the voice or of stringed instruments; and also all the joys, ecstasies, beings, vitalities, felicities, origins and descents, appertaining to all existence and animation. . . . Co-impulsive with the blessed were all animated beings, and God placed them in their innate order and primitive state, within the expanse of felicity,[1] but He Himself existed in the expanse of felicity, where the blessed perceived Him in one communion of glory, without secrecy, without number and without species, that could be ascertained, save essential Light, essential Love and essential Power, for the good of all existencies and vitalities. Then the maxim, 'God and Enough' became established as the basis of truth and oral tradition, and it was the second principle of all realities and sciences transmitted by memory."

(Iolo M.S.

The sacred symbol of the British Gorsedd, the three rays or rods, survive in two forms, in the three "feathers" of the Prince of Wales, and in the "Broad Arrow" of the Government. When Edward III refounded on the Windsor Table Mound the British King Arthur's Order of the Round Table as a reward for those knights who had won for him his victories in France, he adopted the Gorsedd symbol, the sign of spiritual and temporal power of the ancient Keltic kings and priests, as the cognizance of his son, the Black Prince. In the form of three ostrich feathers, the three golden rays have been borne from that time by successive Princes of Wales. As a mark of the Royal Household, they first appear in 1386, and after 1693 were stamped on all Government stores. In our own day, we find the Awen, or Holy Wings, stamped by the Ordnance Survey as a landmark (in the form

---

[1] The Kymric word "Cylch" (circle) is rendered "expanse" in some instances in this translation, the reason being that "circle" is far too limited a term for the residence of the Ominpotent Deity. "Cylch" is Druidically used merely in the sense that state is applied in the expressions—state of felicity, state of infinitude, and state of inchoation—except that it is the symbol of Eternity.

of the Broad Arrow) alike upon solitary mountain peak and kerbstone of crowded alley—the sacred symbol that pro· claims from generation to generation the national faith in the eternal overshadowing of the Divine Wings.

The sign is still sacred among at least half of mankind. It is called the "Sul" throughout Judea. In India it is found employed as a caste mark, the trisul; "and his name shall be in their foreheads." In earliest days every Druid wore the symbol of the ineffable name of the Deity, in gold rays on the front of his linen mitre.

Proceeded by the Regalia of the Order, the members assemble in the market-place, and, marshalled in procession according to their different degrees, wend their way to the Circle. The Arch-Druid, an impressive figure, takes up his position besides the Maen Llogan, raised above the others. Like the High Priest of old, he is clad in white, and wears a golden crescent-shaped breast-plate, symbolic of the Ark or Sacred Boat. He wears a crown of bronze oak leaves round the linen cap upon his head, representing the sacred tree of the ancient Druids. The Druid priests, like their chief, are clad in white, the Bards in blue, symbolic of celestial love, the Ovates in green, signifying the growth of the human intelligence in the circle of the arts and sciences.

The Welsh Bards thus characterize the Druidical Orders in reference to their costume. They describe the Bards as "wearers of the long blue robes"; the Ovates as "having a place in the assembly with their robes of bright green"; and the Druids as the "splendid race-wearers of gold chains—the eminently white."

So conservative is the Order that to this day the same coloured vestments continue to be worn.

Nor must we omit to describe the magnificent Regalia of the Eisteddfod borne in the procession of the Order, before the Arch-Druid. In commemoration of the late Queen's Jubilee the original Regalia, which had disappeared, was re· placed on traditional lines under the direction of Professor Herkomer. Next to the Sword, surmounted by its crystal and emblematic dove, the most striking object is the Hirlas Horn of most ancient symbolism and significance. The Hirlas bore three attributes, viz. authority or might, the loud voice of the sun and its beneficent effects of causing abundance upon the earth. The Hirlas was the chief emblem of the strength of the Creator through the sun, which, at the time of the institution of the Order, rose in Taurus. The sun's rays were represented by the horns of a buffalo pattern. In Welsh, a horn is called "corn," and a crown is called a "coron." In the Bible the horn is alluded to as the emblem of might and power and as the cause of the juice in fruits. The Hirlas Horn was used by the Druids as a sacramental vessel, out of which they drank the first fruits of the sacred Apples, viz. Cider, and afterwards wine, and as each drank out of the Hirlas Horn he bowed to the sun his thanksgiving. One of the Bards of the Neath Valley alludes to the ceremony. There is no doubt our custom of drinking healths is a survival of the holy ancient Bardic custom. In this we have also the origin of passing the wine in the path of the sun. The most historic Hirlas Horn was presented to Henry Tudor by Sir Rhys ap Thomas and the Gentlemen of Wales, who had been instrumental in placing him upon the throne of his Keltic ancestors. It is reputed to be the work of Torrigiano, the Italian artist, who designed the Tomb of Henry VII in Westminster Abbey, and is now in the possession of the Earl of Cawdor, a lineal descendant of Sir Rhys ap Thomas.

When all have taken up their respective positions within the circle, four long blasts of a silver trumpet announce the fact to the vast concourse. The Arch-Druid, with uplifted, outstretched arms, then proceeds to open the congress with the Gorsedd prayer, reputed to be as old as the Institution.

The translation of this magnificent invocation gives no sort of idea of the rhythmic grandeur of the sublime utterances, as petition after petition is poured forth in the sonorous tones of the Welsh language. With Arnold we may find here, and in Keltic literature generally, "traces of a kinship, and that the most essential sort of kinship, spiritual kinship, between us and the Kelt, of which we never dreamed."

GWEDDI'R ORSEDD (The Gorsedd Prayer).

Dyro Dduw dy Nawdd;
Ag yn Nawdd, Nerth;
Ag yn Nerth, Deall;
Ag yn Neall, Gwybod;
Ac yngwybod, Gwybod y Cyfiawn;
Ag yngwybod y Cyfiawn, ei Garu;
Ag o Garu, Caru pob Hanfod;
Ag ymhob Hanfod, Caru Duw.
Duw a phob Daioni.

Translation

Grant, O God, Thy Protection;
And in Protection, Strength;
And in Strength, Understanding;
And in Understanding, Knowledge;
And in Knowledge, the Knowledge of Justice;
And in that Knowledge of Justice, the Love of it;
And in that Love, the Love of all Existences;
And in the Love of all Existences, the Love of God.
God and all Goodness.

At the moment of prayer all the twelve Bards, the guardians of the twelve stones, bow the head towards the Arch-Druid, and the resemblance of the scene to the Great White Throne described in the Revelation is most startling. The mysterious reverence, awe and silence that holds the vast multitude spellbound, whilst the historic "solemnities" of the Order are proceeded with, gives one an idea of the influence that such "solemn assemblies" must have exercised upon the nation at large in past times.

"DUW A DIGON"
(*God and Enough*)

Or

"Y GWIR YN ERBYN Y BYD"
(*Truth against the World*)

APPENDICES A AND B

BY THE REV. JOHN GRIFFITH
THE INTERPRETER OF THE PHAESTUS DISC-CALENDAR

THE INTERPRETATION OF PREHISTORIC MONUMENTS, ILLUSTRATED BY THE MONUMENTS OF AVEBURY, THE INTERRELATION OF MOUNDS, AND THE ALIGNMENTS OF ANCIENT ROADS, IN THE DISTRICT OF LONDON

A

FACTS of measurement, and some reasonable deductions from such facts, will occupy almost exclusively the attention of the reader of these notes, if after this forewarning any reader will be disposed to read any further what is commonly relegated to the Dryasdusts.

First, something should be said of the method of analysing measures of monuments by which certain facts are elicited. The most pressing problem of prehistoric archæology is to find a reliable time-measuring criterion. For the prehistoric period, archæological time is largely geological time, time measured truly by sequences of phenomena, which sequences, however, are difficult to convert into terms of years. Conclusions based on the accumulation of deposits are apt to be widely different, even when put forth by experts, as in the case of Knossos, Crete, where the difference in expert estimates is 7,000 years.

Many archæologists are duly impressed with the variability of the best archæological criteria where no historical landmark of any kind guides the inquirer. A conviction of the kind reveals the open mind, as well as the policy of the open door for a better system of time-measuring antiquities.

It is certain, in any case, that the solution of the problem referred to will depend on exact measurements. It is equally

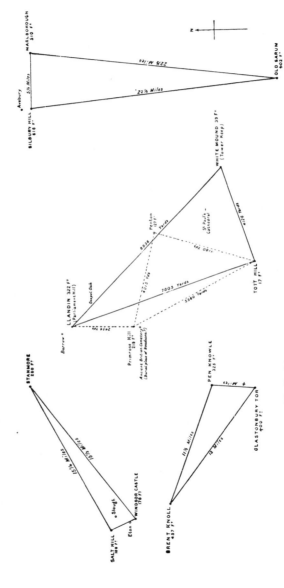

PLAN OF THE INTER-RELATION OF MOUNDS.

(By Stanford.)

146

certain that some safe method must be found by which the accuracy of the measurements may be tested. That method, I venture with confidence to say, has been found. Individual measures of an ancient monument are component parts of a symmetrical whole, and the symmetry disclosed by dove-tailing the measures represents the architect's mind. The method is practically infallible, and in numberless instances it has served to correct and to reconstruct defective measures. There remains only the main problem to be faced, namely, the interpretation of individual measures. It is conclusively and clearly proved that the individual measures of an ancient monument represents celestial distances or angles of the circle, and that the basal measure, differing only with the latitude, and the lapse of time in the same latitude, which measure is the apparent distance between the sun's positions, as measured on the horizon, at Midsummer and Christmas, the longest and the shortest days. Wherever the architectural symmetry can be made out, the fundamental measure reveals itself, that is, the astronomy of the builders is revealed, based as it was on local phenomena at the time the building was erected. The inter-solstitial measure recorded in a structure may be compared with the corresponding present measure for the latitude. The rate of change in such a measure is known with sufficient precision, that, in most cases where accurate measures are obtainable, a prehistoric date may be fixed to a century or two.

What I have briefly outlined is a new applied science, the application of astronomy to the interpretation of ancient monuments. Founded by Sir Norman Lockyer, K.C.B., the discoverer of helium and the great authority on the constitution of the sun, it has just reached its majority before hardly a baker's dozen have learnt its uses. It is necessary to explain, however, that Sir Norman has confined himself to teaching us how to interpret angular measures, such as the alignments or directions of monuments. It has been given to the present writer to discover, or re-discover, that a system of astronomy, which Sir Norman Lockyer had theoretically derived from British monuments, is embodied in the traditional lore of Welsh and Irish bards, and it has become very clear that the monuments and the traditional lore of a people interpret each other.

I must also explain that, as far as I know, I am alone responsible for saying that the astronomy of a monument can be derived from linear measures of length, as well as from angular measures, tape as well as compass measures, and that the fundamental measure of the symmetry is the inter-solstitial distance. Linear and angular measures always agree as component measures of the same symmetry, and such being the case the task of analysing a given set of measures has been greatly simplified.

If the astronomical method of dating monuments is at all scientific, the dimensions of monuments in the same latitudes should be generally similar. In the tropics, a range of a dozen latitudes makes but a slight difference in the requisite astronomical measures, and the monument measures of Egypt and Mexico should tally closely. In both countries, the inter-solstitial measure is 50° and something, and the monuments of both countries give us varying increments. All Americanists know that the Mexican calendar is based on the number 52, and the excellent measures I have seen of monuments at Palenque, Chichen Itza, Mitla, and Xaaga, in Mexico, yield variations of the round measure 50°. Such a required and actual latitude correspondence indicates the significance of the fact that the basal dimension of the Teotihuacan pyramid, Mexico, is exactly the same as that of one of the pyramids of Dashūr, Egypt, which is 700 feet square. Another Dashūr pyramid is 350 feet square, half the size of the pyramids named. Again, another Dashūr pyramid is 343 feet square, which as 686 feet, a full-grown pyramid, would agree with the culminating measure of a temple symmetry at Xaaga, Mexico, which is 686 feet and 8 inches, that is to say, if the latter monument had been laid out as a pyramid, that pyramid would have been just double the size of a Dashūr pyramid. I have seen it stated also that the pyramidal structure at Cholula, Mexico, is twice as large in base as the Great Pyramid of Egypt.

Moving higher north, I have been genuinely startled at finding in measures of some structures recently excavated at

Pueblo, New Mexico, the available symmetrical measures of
Diana's temple at Ephesus, and of Noah's Ark, the origin of
the last-mentioned measures being clearly traceable to the
latitude of Nineveh. In this latitude correspondence, the
solar measure is 60 something; hence the sexagesimal system
of numeration which is commonly ascribed to the Chaldeans.

Apart altogether from the possibility of finding in such facts
a safe criterion for dating monuments, a classification of
monuments by measure reveals the stubborn fact or law that
culture is very largely a matter of latitude, and even as a
matter of latitude the determining factor is not so much the
climate as some astronomical phenomena with which races in
the same latitude the world over would be similarly impressed.
Again, a people's calendar has always been the vertebral
column of its organized culture, notably organized religion,
and in the study of comparative culture, the influence of
latitude, with all it implies, should be considered with the
innate endowments of man and ethnological characteristics.

A classification of monuments by measure first reveals a
general latitude correspondence. The maximum measure or
dimension is to be regarded as the multiple of measures involved in the structural symmetry, and I come now to the
first of a surprising series of facts relating to the group of
monuments to which attention is here invited.

The maximum dimension of Avebury, which doubtless was,
with its minor circles and avenues, the greatest British megalithic monument, is the same as that of the ten-lined avenue
at Kermario, in the Carnac district of Brittany, which seems
to be the finest of the Breton avenues. The total length of the
ten rows of the latter is about 1,250 yards. The diameter of
the great circle at Avebury is stated to be 1,250 feet, which,
multiplied by 3, shows a circumference equal to the total
length of the Breton avenue.

In theory, monuments of the same measures in the same
latitude are to be regarded as contemporaneous. As the
latitude of Kermario is about 48° 30′ N., and that of Avebury
51° 30′ N., we have further to consider whether a difference of
three degrees of latitude, in such a case, is convertible into
terms of years. The same consideration applies to the Egyp-

tian and Mexican monuments referred to. They are not exactly in the same latitude though near enough for the correspondence of the maximum measures to arrest one's attention. The maximum measure, however, is not to be relied upon alone, as it would have been possible to express different sets of component measures in such a figure, say, as 700 feet, or 1,250 yards. Some, at least, of the component measures must be ascertained at each site before the contemplated symmetry can be made out with certainty. Yet were it not for the tendency of maximum measures to group themselves by latitude, more convincing facts would have remained undetected.

If the leading figures of Avebury and Kermario represent the same set of astronomical measures, that is, approximately, the difference in latitude must be considered as a difference in time. It is practically certain that the fundamental measures are about the same in both monuments, and that being the case, to be further made out, I may as well state here what differences in latitude we want to convert into terms of years. It will be shown that the astronomical measures indicated at Avebury are now true of latitude 53° N., or that of Derby, that the astronomical or physical conditions have moved northwards $1\frac{1}{2}°$ since Avebury was constructed. But the pristine conditions at Kermario now obtain near the latitude of Avebury, an interesting coincidence. Kermario has moved to Avebury, travelling 3° or so, where its ten rows in one line would fit the enormous bank of the great circle, and that at a time when we are, in my estimation, about succeeding in understanding the structural principles of that vanished world-wonder. Whether Kermario is twice as ancient as Avebury, as the latitude difference indicates, is a matter I am not going into without fuller knowledge of the Breton monument, but I must state the grounds upon which that monument is to be considered with Avebury, apart from the coincidence of the maximum measures.

The first and most important measure to be made is that of a leading alignment or direction, the measure above all else which is commonly spoken of as the "orientation" of a structure. Mr. Worsfold, in his useful work, *The French Stonehenge,* gives oriented plans of the leading Breton avenues. The lines at Kermario are straight, but not exactly parallel; they open out towards the south-west. As a consequence, we get three angular measures, which I have made out with a protractor as follows:

The outermost north line . . 64° N.E.–S.W.
    ,,   ,,   south line . 61° 30′ N.E.–S.W.
Difference between the measures . . 2° 30′.

The ends of the avenue are truncated, but in the plan some converging point at a measurable distance north-east must have been contemplated. From such a point the ten rows served the purpose of dividing an angle of 2° 30′, on the south-west skyline, into nine equal parts, or units, say of about 16′ 40″.

Sir Norman Lockyer gives us the theoretical conditions for lat. 51° 30′ (*Stonehenge*, 2nd ed., p. 350), and the following comparison will indicate the significance of the Kermario alignments :

May–August sun, N. 62° E. Kermario N. 61° 30′ E.
Nov.–Feb. sun, S. 64° 12′ E. Kermario S. 64° W.

Considering the ancient importance of the alignments, as marking the half-year points of the farmer's year, and the remarkably close agreement of the derived with the normal figures, it seems to me impossible to question the obvious fact that Kermario was designed in agreement with conditions which now obtain in the latitude of Avebury. At the present time the corresponding measures at Kermario must be about 65° and 67°.

Kermario, at any rate, in its maximum measure and its May-November alignments, serves as the first key to Avebury. Sir Norman Lockyer gives the following azimuths or directions which justify the introduction of Kermario into the discussion:

The Cove at Avebury . . . . N. 65° E.
Beckhampton Avenue . . . . N. 64° E.
North-east road . . . . N. 64° E.

As the skyline north-east is 2° high, the normal measure of the May-August sunrise would be about 61° or less. It was doubtless the leading measure at Avebury as well as Kermario, and its repetition in three separate alignments is a noteworthy fact.

That such measures at Avebury, as well as elsewhere, were intended to be symmetrical is at once apparent by comparing the two best angular measures now obtainable, those of the two great avenues. The Beckhampton measure leads the rest, and that of the Kennet Avenue, S. 32° E., is half of the leading measure. In searching for as many measures as possible, I find the following decisive alignments shown in the map section utilized by Sir Norman (*Stonehenge*, p. 357). All the roads mentioned radiate from near the centre of the great circle :

North-west road	N. 21° W.
High Street	N. 78° E.
Road south-west of Kennet Avenue .	S. 38° E.

At least ten blocks of building are oriented with reference to the north-west road, and that in parallel lines. It is here to be provisionally assumed that the road-measures preserve the angular values of vanished alignments, and are about the best measures obtainable at Avebury.

Having given the front place to the available angular measures, I select the following as representative of the linear design, gathered from various authorities :

Diameter of the great circle	1,250 or 1,260 feet
,, ,, inner circle . .	325 feet
,, ,, ,, ,, . .	350 feet
Length of Kennet Avenue . . .	1,430 feet
Width ,, ,, ,, . . .	43 feet
Height of some stones . . .	21 feet

With the best angular and linear measures, there is another set of facts to be looked for. If a numerical symmetry was contemplated, the factors or divisors would be, as a rule, specially indicated. Such must have been the use of standing stones ranged in regular distances, and such, I believe, was the origin of number-motives in ancient art. For our present purpose, we must have numbers as well as measures, angular and linear. It is in the harmony of the three categories, angle, line, and number, that the real secret of the monuments lies. As this triple alliance has no name, as far as I know, the harmony or combination may be described as an arithmometric or number-measure harmony.

Our third want is suppled by authorities on Avebury in the numbers of stones forming circles. The great circle consisted of one hundred stones; one of the inner circles had thirty and the other twelve. It is seen at once that the inner circles were complementary. Where a circle consisted of stones fixed at regular distances, the obvious purpose must have been to divide the circle of 360° into sections corresponding to the number of the stones. It is here assumed without a comment that the builders of Avebury divided the celestial circle just as we do. The number-motives at Avebury marked off segments of that circle as follows:

$$100 \text{ stones} = 3° \ 36'.$$
$$30 \quad ,, \quad = 12°.$$
$$12 \quad ,, \quad = 30°.$$

Wherever any number-motives can be made out to a certainty, equal certainty belongs to the derived angular measures as being exactly what the architect had in mind, such numbers being more to be relied upon than any actual angular or linear measures.

A circle like the 12-stone one at Avebury served as the prototype of the present conventional Gorsedd circle of the Welsh bards, which consists of 12 stones at regular intervals of 30°.

We have now fairly good materials for examining the arithmometric properties of Avebury. At the outset, it must be borne in mind that we have there at least three different monuments to investigate, which could hardly have been erected at one and the same time. The greatest of all, the great circle, is shown archæologically to be a later structure than the avenues which are connected with the inner circles, the great bank, as Sir Norman Lockyer points out, having been constructed so as to obstruct both the avenues. Each monument was doubtlessly independently symmetrical.

The length, breadth, and direction of the Kennet Avenue being given, its symmetry should disclose itself. Its direction is numerically half of that of the other avenue. Its width 43 multiplied by the azimuth 32, gives its approximate length as 1,376 feet, 54 feet too short. This fact, supported by analogous facts, suggests that neither 43 nor 32 is quite correct. There were minutes, and perhaps seconds, to be reckoned. As a general rule, a measure with increments or fractions was multiplied into a convenient integer, or a whole number, and this may have been the chief reason why some enormously long monuments were erected. Then, again, the monument-builders divided and multiplied by integers, and number-motives are always integers. Assuming that 1,430 is a multiple of both the width and the azimuth of the avenue, and finding that its length is divisible by 11, the method of multiplication reveals itself. The direction is something over 32, and the width over 43; therefore the factors were 33 and 44. Dividing 1,430 by 44 gives the azimuth as 32° 30′, and dividing the same number by 33 gives the width as 43 feet 4 inches, to be astronomically expressed as 43° 20′. The dual result will appear quite justified as we proceed.

We have already learnt:

(1) The ancient method of multiplying such figures as 43° 20′ and 32° 30′ into a maximum figure.

(2) That the length of the avenue is its azimuth multiplied by its width.

(3) That the numerical unit of the arithmometric harmony is 1 foot = 1 degree.

The third lesson is taught wherever measures of ancient monuments are available. The second may prove to be a fairly general rule, at least, in the sense that the azimuth and width of a monument, multiplied, supply a multiple which involves the whole structural symmetry. This interesting rule I have not observed elsewhere before writing these notes, but a hasty search for an analogy has resulted in finding one in point. It is supplied in the famous monument at Callernish, in the island of Lewes. Sir Norman Lockyer, quoting Anderson, gives the length of the north-east avenue as about 270 feet, its width as 27 feet, and its azimuth, as supplied by Sir Henry James, as N. 9° E. Here, again, it is hardly likely that even one of the measures is quite correct, and only by the rarest of chances could an astronomical measure be an integer. But with the worked-out example of the Kennet Avenue before us, the Callernish measures, as we have them, may be accepted as confirmatory evidence of the rule under notice. If the azimuth were 10, the symmetry would be complete, $27 \times 10 = 270$.

The derived azimuth of the Kennet Avenue, 32° 30', agrees as half of that of the Cove, 65°. Similarly, the azimuth of the north-west road, roughly measured as 21°, is practically half of the width value, 43° 20'.

Experience in examining monument measures teaches that the leading measures are categorically the same, differing only with the place and time. The solstices, equinox, and the farmer's quarter-days are always and everywhere indicated. Always and everywhere, also, clock-stars, the time-keepers of the night, are provided for. The arithmometric method of analysis, rather, the symmetrical requirements of a monument, show that stellar measures, or measures north or south of the sun's half-yearly track along the horizon, were co-ordinated symmetrically with the solar quarterly and half-quarterly points. Thus, the azimuth of the Kennet Avenue is to a point south-east below the southern end of the sun's course at Christmas. Therefore, the avenue is primarily a stellar one. Yet its azimuth is numerically half of that of the primarily solar Beckhampton Avenue and the Cove. In this way, stellar measures are to a large extent categorically related to solar ones.

In this attempt at interpreting and reconstructing ruinated temples by tricks of figures, it is absolutely necessary to find in the monuments themselves rules which govern the inquiry. As the number 1,430 is divisible by 11, that divisor has given us figures for both the azimuth and the width which agree remarkably well with the measures actually made. Other hypothetical or theoretical measures must be derived in the same way, that is, the measures must be multiples of .11.

1,430 ÷ 11 = 130, the height of Silbury Hill, 130 feet! The result is twice the azimuth of the Cove, and four times that of the avenue. The height of Silbury will be seen to be the harmonic unit of Kennet Avenue.

1,430 ÷ 22 = 65, the azimuth of the Cove and, probably, of the Beckhampton Avenue.

1,430 ÷ 55 = 26, the right angle of the latter avenue.

1,430 ÷ 66 = 21° 40', half of the avenue's width; also the azimuth of the north-west road.

77 is not a divisor of 1,430.

1,430 ÷ 88 = 16° 15', half the azimuth.

1,430 ÷ 99 = 14° 26' 40", one-third of the azimuth. The right angle to this measure, 75° 46' 40", divided by 2 = 37° 46' 40", is the azimuth of the road south-west of Kennet Avenue, which I have roughly measured as 38°. This last measure is decisive as to the purpose of the great circle, as will be seen.

1,430 ÷ 110 = 13. We now get 77 in as the right angle, which is probably the corrected azimuth of High Street.

With the possible exception of the last, it is seen that every measure derived by 11 is duplicated in an actual measure made. The unit numbers of the avenue are found to be 5, 11, 13.

Treating the longest measures or figures as multiples of astronomical measures under 90°, it will be seen that the longer the measure the more accurate should be the component measures. A mistake of an inch where 2 feet is concerned would amount to an error of 50 feet in adding up to 1,000, while it is hardly likely that those who measured the length of the Kennet Avenue as 1,430 feet erred at such a rate. Even a mistake of 10 or 20 feet in such a number would not affect the distinctive character of the harmonic measures.

Dealing as I am with facts of a somewhat novel character, it is necessary to present them in such a way as to produce an impression of their reality. The longest monument in Britain, apparently, is the Cursus at Stonehenge. It is stated to be

10,000 feet long. Sir Norman Lockyer has made out the direction of the Cursus to be N. 82° E. The enormous length, in feet, is the azimuth or direction multiplied by 122, the half of which, 61, being in all probability the measure at the time of construction of the May-August sunrise, just as the length of the Kennet Avenue is the azimuth 32° 30′ multiplied by 44, the latter figure to be roughly connected with the summer solstice. The azimuth of the Cursus as derived from its length is 81° 58′ 1″, with fractions of a second, showing that the measure given by Sir Norman seems to be correct to within two minutes of arc. As the width of the Cursus is the same as the diameter of one of the Avebury circles, 350 feet, the evidence of design is unmistakable.

The orientation of the Cursus is repeated in the Merrivale Avenue, Dartmoor, which is 1,143 feet long. It consists of two rows which, as in some Breton avenues, are not exactly parallel. The azimuth of the north row is given by Sir Norman as N. 82° E., and the south row, N. 80° 30′ E. The azimuth derived from the length is 1,143÷14=81° 38′ 34″, with fractions, and the mean of the two azimuths given is 81° 15′. The result is satisfactory enough as proof of our arithmometric rule.

The Kennet Avenue is connected with a circle, the diameter of which is given as 325 feet. The number is the avenue azimuth 32° 30′ multiplied by 10. It is also the width of the avenue divided into 19 parts of 21° 40′, the azimuth of the north-west road. So far the circle appears to be but another combination of the two fundamental measures of the avenue. The real *raison d'être* of the circle discloses itself when compared with its companion circle. The diameter of the latter is given as 350 feet. Dividing that number by 4, we have 87° 30′, half of which is 43° 45′, which at once reminds us of the angular value of the avenue's width 43° 20′. The figures could not have been exactly the same, as the structures are independent of each other. One is surely older than the other.

Now the cardinal measure of the west circle is 43° 45′, which is also, 25 minutes less, a fundamental measure of the east circle and its avenue. Dividing the diameter 325 of the east circle by 4, we have 81° 15′ as the cardinal measure of that circle, the half of which 40° 37′ 30″, is evidently the winter complement of the circle avenue measure 43° 20′. The latter must be treated provisionally as the amplitude of the sun, or its distance north of the east point, at the summer solstice, and the former as the winter solstice amplitude. Though that circle-avenue supplies us with both amplitudes, the distinguishing measure of the circle is the winter solstitial measure, and, therefore, it must be regarded as the winter circle.

I assume that the height of the horizon north-east is about the same as observed from both circles; therefore, the difference between the two summer solstice measures, assuming the approximate accuracy of the linear measures, should indicate a difference in date. The solstitial amplitude is diminishing at an ascertained rate. The larger the amplitude figures appear to be the remoter the period. A summer solstice measure always supplies a downward date-limit, and the corresponding winter measure an upward limit. If, therefore, the face values of the measures could be timed, the average would be an approximate date.

The numerical difference between 43° 20′ and 40° 37′ 30″ =2′ 42° 30″, is less than the theoretical normal difference would be, on account of inequalities of skyline. Though the winter amplitude of the west or summer circle is still to be made out, its relation to the summer measure may be approximately guessed. Treating the two sets of figures, they are here placed together with the theoretical figures for latitudes 53° and 51° 30′, as given by Sir Norman Lockyer.

	West Circle	East Circle	Lat. 53°	Lat. 51° 30
Summer solstice	43° 45′	43° 20′	43° 20′	41° 18′
Winter solstice	(41° 2′ 30″)	40° 37′ 30″	40° 20′	38° 25′

It is seen that the theoretical difference for latitude 53° is just 3°. It must have been slightly more at the Avebury circles. Where the north-east skyline is higher than the south-east one the mean solstitial amplitude would be less than the normal. Also, it should be remembered that I use linear measures without a certificate of their correctness.

The physical or astronomical conditions indicated by the

two circles obtain at the present time somewhat higher north than latitude 53° or that of Derby, that is, the conditions have moved northwards over $1\frac{1}{2}$°. Is the west circle older than the east one by the time value of 25 minutes' difference in the summer amplitude?

Sir Norman Lockyer finds the Kennet Avenue to be oriented to the star Alpha Centauri, in 3500 B.C. The azimuth he gives as S. 32° E.; which, as in other cases cited, agrees practically with the arithmometric azimuth. Usually where the solstitial amplitude is unknown, there is uncertainty attached to mere star-dates, as the leading stars exchange positions at long intervals of time. But the cult and period of Alpha Centauri, as a monument star, has been so clearly and convincingly made out by Sir Norman, both in Egypt and Britain, that to detect its employment by the monument-builders is remarkably easy, that is, after Sir Norman has opened our eyes. Where a star of rapid motion is indicated with fair certainty in a monument, the date can be made out to a much narrower margin than by the best examination of what solar values may be derived from "rude stone monuments."

There is a mass of cumulative evidence, geological and monumental, going to show that the Megalithic Age, so to speak, or Neolithic Age, did not commence in Britain much before 4000 B.C. During that age or period, monuments oriented to a low south-east point, which may be found from the Lake District to Brittany, unmistakably indicate Alpha Centauri, for the reason that during that period there is no other leading star to be considered in that quarter. In keeping with the geological or climatic evidence, Sir Norman finds its earliest indication in the Challacombe Avenue in Cornwall, in 3600 B.C., and the cult reached Shap, Westmorland, in 3400 B.C. By 3000 B.C., the uplands of Glamorgan, at elevations of from 1,300 to 1,700 feet above the level of the sea, became habitable, and there we find two avenues, and indications of a third, oriented to Alpha Centauri.

It is a remarkable fact that the brightest star in the constellation of the Centauri, the cult of which in Britain seems to have been co-extensive with the Neolithic Age, which might very well be called the Centaurian Age in Britain, ceased to be of use in our latitudes at the close of the Neo-lithic Age. Its later use was as a southern clock-star and as herald of the November festival. It retreated southward, and, according to Sir Norman's list, its latest monument is a Breton one, dated 1700 B.C.

To those who are familiar with the facts of the case, the Centaurian date of the Kennet Avenue is so well supported that it may be used as means of fixing the approximate time-value of the indicated solstitial amplitude. The solstitial table I have given shows a difference of 2° 2′ between the summer amplitude indicated in the east circle and the present amplitude. The stellar date is 3500 B.C., or a period of 5,400 years. The rate per quarter of a degree would be about 675 years. At such a rate, the difference of 25 minutes between the west and east circles, in amplitude value, would make the west circle about a thousand years earlier than the east circle, say, 4500 B.C. But the best information we can expect through such playing with solstitial values is a general idea of the sun's whereabouts at a period which is well defined by a Centaurian date, and an indication of the priority in date of the west circle.

With the date 3500 B.C. considered as well established for the Kennet Avenue, we can now consider other stellar evi-dence in point. We have derived from the east circle-avenue measures of the summer and winter solstices, and of Alpha Centauri. Other measures, hypothetically derived, agree with observed measures at Avebury.

The orientation of the Kennet Avenue is manifestly a stellar one. It is to be noted that the Beckhampton Avenue is con-nected with the west circle on its south-west side, and though the azimuth 64° N.E.-S.W., with a hill of 2° north-east, would have certainly marked May-day and Lammas, what seems probable is, that the avenue was designed to mark the setting of a star in the south-west in either May or August. It is re-markable that the outlooks of both avenues are to the south, and that one of the uses of the east avenue was to mark the rising of the star-herald of the November festival. The avenue by Arthur's Stone, Gower, was designed to mark both the May and November festivals.

Alignments at right angles to each other are always to be looked for, and such alignments are specially provided in stone circles. The right angle to the Centaurian azimuth would be 58°. Though that measure is not included in those observed at Avebury, it is categorically correct, for one thing because it is twice the normal amplitude of the May-August sunrise at such time as we are contemplating. The star indicated would be probably a north one, which heralded that sunrise.

Deducting three degrees on account of the skyline elevation, the declination of 55° would be about 20°, and the star indicated is Spica, the brightest in the constellation of the Virgin, and the date about 3750 B.C. Spica represented the virgin-goddess in August, and Sir Norman Lockyer has shown, in his *Dawn of Astronomy*, quoting the late Mr. Penrose, how extensively the cult of Spica was involved in the construction of temples in the Ægean, notably the temples of Diana.

It is rather curious that the width of the Kennet Avenue, of southern significance, should seem to be the amplitude of the summer solstice. The width is 43 feet. I gather from Wilkinson's remark that the width of the Gower Avenue referred to is 49 feet, which, he observes, is six feet more than that of the Kennet Avenue. The Gower width seems to be the azimuth of the winter solstice, which is indicated in the Kennet Avenue as 49° 22′ 30″, being the complement of the cardinal measure of the east circle.

The reason why a distinctively winter circle-avenue specially provides a summer or north measure will now be seen. The skyline elevation south-east is given by Sir Norman as a little under one degree. The measure then, as an azimuth, say, would be 44° 30′, declination 25° 30′, star, Sirius, in 3600 B.C.

The period which is repeatedly indicated at Avebury is practically that of the pyramid times in Egypt, when Sirius became the herald of the summer solstice and New Year's Day in Egypt. The association of the star with the summer solstice at Avebury seems to be clearly revealed, though, as far as I can make out, it is the position of the solstitial star, more than the actual position of the sun at the summer solstice in 3600 B.C. that is revealed.

There is now hardly a question as to the inclusion of Alpha

Centauri, Spica, and Sirius in the astronomical scheme of the east circle-avenue. It is the half of the measure of Sirius that is probably preserved in the direction of the north-west road.

We have seen that Spica's measure is the right angle to that of Alpha Centauri, and twice the amplitude of the festival day in August with which the cult of Spica is known to have connected. One of the measures regularly derived by 11 from 1,430 is 14° 26′ 40″, which, multiplied by 3, seems to be the normal measure of Sirius in 3600 B.C. The right angle to the former measure is 75° 33′ 20″, the half of which, 37° 46′ 40″, seems to be preserved in that of the road south-west of Kennet Avenue, a measure to be further discussed. Theoretically, the right angle of the latter measure was utilized. It is 52° 13′ 20″, which, as a north measure at right angle to the direction of the said road, would, less skyline value, be about 49°, or near the normal measure of the winter solstice azimuth. Now this measure should give us a north star warner of the winter solstice, in harmony with the connexion of Sirius with the summer solstice.

The declination of 49° would be about 23° 30′, and the star indicated is Capella in 3500 B.C. This result appears to be a very striking one. We have really to consider whether in such monuments exact conventional solar positions are marked, or star-positions near such points, which once would have exactly coincided. A star like Capella could have appeared as fairly coincidental with the solstice only during one generation, but as in later times it seems to have served for a long period as a February star, there seems to be no reason to doubt but that it was for a long time a winter solstice star. At the same time, the measures 52°, reduced to 49°, and 44°, increased from 43° 20′, seem to be very near the solstitial measures required in the case.

It is very likely that the rising of Sirius was observed diagonally at the Kennet Avenue, close to which was another avenue or *via sacra* at right angles to the rising point of Capella. The manifestly artificial symmetry disclosed appears here in close touch with nature, associated as the figures are with the great turning movements of nature, the solstices. It is true to nature to find the solstitial star marked in a quarter opposite to the solstice. At Midsummer the northern stars are greatly obscured, and at Christmas the southern stars are considerably so. At Avebury, the Christmas star appeared in the north-east, and the Midsummer star in the south-east.

I find so far no clear indication of the equinox, and the reason may be that the equinotical star did not quite coincide with that point. As I have made out that the east circle and avenue were primarily stellar monuments, it is reasonable to suppose that the west circle and avenue were of the same character. The cardinal measure of the west circle, 87° 30′, which seems to be approximately twice the amplitude at one time of the summer solstice, would fit the equinox with some height to the east. Antares was an equinoctial star in 3700 B.C. A hundred years later it was about a degree south of east, and its azimuth in all probability was 87° 30′, S.E.

The east circle is the azimuth of the Kennet Avenue multiplied by ten. The west circle of 350 feet, divided by ten, yields the measure 35°, which is to be assumed to be a stellar one. Taken as 36° for a south measure, the declination would be about 29° 30′, Alpha Centauri in 4000 B.C. At that time Antares was between 2° and 3° north of east, and marked the *apparent* equinox.

Now as we found an earlier Centaurian date in the west circle, confirmed by an Antares date, it seems highly probable that the half of the Antares azimuth, 43° 45′, is a Sirian measure, if not an actual solstitial measure. Treating that measure as an amplitude at 42°, the declination would be about 26° 30′, Sirius in 4000 B.C.

We have now the following star dates for each circle-avenue:

East Circle				West Circle			
Alpha Centauri	.	3500	B.C.	Alpha Centauri	.	4000	B.C.
Sirius .	. .	3600	,,	Sirius	. . .	,,	,,
Spica	. .	3750	,,	Antares .	. .	,,	,,
Capella	. .	3500	,,				
Mean date	.	3587	B.C.				

The net results of this enquiry so far seem to be as follows:

1. There seems to be no feature of the two circles and avenues examined so strikingly as the harmony wrought by means of two measures in each case. It is in fact the leading archæological feature of the whole site.

2. Measures which were unquestionably contemplated in the design yield harmonious stellar dates, in keeping with general indications of the solstitial range within which stellar dates are to be looked for.

THE INTERRELATION OF MOUNDS.

OLD SARUM GROUP.

Silbury Hill–Marlborough . . .	90°, or East-west.
Silbury Hill–Old Sarum . . .	6° 30′ N.W.–S.E.
Old Sarum–Marlborough . .	6° 30′ N.E.–S.W.
Angle at Old Sarum	13°
Angle at both Silbury and Marlborough	83° 30′.

83° 30′ ÷ 2   = 41° 45′, = amplitude of summer solstice.

83° 30′ N., dec.	4° 30′,	Aldebaran, 1300 B.C.
„ „ S., dec.	3° 30′,	Antares, 3100 B.C.
6° 30′ N., dec.	36° 37′,	Arcturus, 1350 B.C.
		Capella, 900 B.C.

The diagram presents an ideal star-clock. The date favoured by the evidence is 1325 B.C., when Arcturus rose, as observed from Old Sarum, over Marlborough at right angles to the setting point of Aldebaran, and when the same star set over Silbury Hill at right angles to the rising point of Aldebaran. One degree of skyline elevation is assumed. The measure 6° 30′ is practically a divisor of all the other measures, and such symmetry is first-class evidence of design.

WINDSOR GROUP.

Salt Hill–Stanmore . .	62° 30′ N.E.–S.W.
Windsor–Stanmore . .	53° 15′ N.E.–S.W.
Windsor–Salt Hill . .	27° 15′ N.W.–S.E.
Angle at Stanmore . .	9° 15′.
Angle at Windsor . .	79°
Angle at Salt Hill . .	90°.

Like Old Sarum, Stanmore is the apex of an equilateral triangle. In the former case, the base of the triangle is the equinox; in the latter case, the base is 27° 15′, which is practically the right angle to 62° 30′, sunrise in May or sunset in November or both.

27° 15′, dec. 33° 30′, Capella, 1550 B.C.

53° 15′, dec. 20° 30′, Sirius, 1550 B.C.

27° 15′+13° 37′ 30″=40° 52′ 30″=amplitude of the summer solstice?

53° 15′÷2=26° 37′ 30″=right angle, 63° 22′ 30″=May or November.

26° 37′ 30″+13° 18′ 45″=39° 56′ 15″=amplitude of the winter solstice?

The last measure is either the same, with necessary corrections, as 40° 52′ 30″, or the latter is the summer solstice amplitude with a higher skyline. The angle at Stanmore, 9° 15′, may be regarded as a stellar measure like 13° of the Old Sarum group; as a unit, in fact, of the contemplated symmetry. All the Windsor measures are divisible by something near 9. By the same analogy 9° 15′ is a clock-star measure, and its half, 4° 37′ 30″, would correspond to 6° 13′ of the other group, giving us Arcturus at an earlier date to suit the Capella and Sirius dates. We have, therefore, three stellar dates agreeing in 1500 B.C. as the date of the Windsor group. Here, again, the numerical symmetry is real evidence, the more telling because it is different to the Old Sarum one, as with an earlier date it was bound to be.

LONDON MOUNDS.

MEASURES OF ALIGNMENTS.

Tower–Parliament Hill	. .	46° 45′ N.W.–S.E.
Tower–Tothill	. . .	72° 30′ N.E.–S.W.
Tothill–Parliament Hill	. .	19° 15′ N.W.–S.E.
Tothill–Penton	. .	17° 30′ N.E.–S.W.
Penton–Primrose Hill	. .	76° 45′ N.W.–S.E.
Tothill–Primrose Hill	. .	28° N.W.–S.E.
Primrose Hill–Parliament Hill	.	2° N.W.–S.E.

Angle at Tower	. . .	60° 45′.
Angles at Tothill	. . .	(1) 91°, (2) 9° 15′, (3) 55°.
Angle at Penton	. . .	91°.
Angles at Primrose Hill	. .	(1) 48° 45′, (2) 101° 30′.
Angles at Parliament Hill .	.	(1) 21°, (2) 27° 30′.

In each case, one degree of skyline elevation is assumed. The measure 46° 45′+1°=47° 45′ would be the azimuth of the summer solstice, which was marked, in this case as at Avebury, by the rising of a star in the south-east. That star was Sirius about 3250 B.C. The same measure less one degree would mark the setting of Capella about 3150 B.C. The mean date would be 3200 B.C. The north measure of the summer solstice is given as 48° 45′, less one degree 47° 45′. This correspondence is truly remarkable, and made still more so by a Welsh legend. Blessed Brân commanded his followers to cut off his head. "And take my head," said he, "and bear it even unto the White Mount, in London, and bury it there, with the face towards France." (*The Mabinogion*, Nutt's edition, p. 39.) The legend of Brân is undoubtedly largely astronomical. There is, for instance, Brân's injunction about keeping a door in a certain direction closed. I have always thought, but could not make it out until I saw the diagram of the London mounds, that the burial injunction has reference to the leading astronomical measure worked into the legend. The Parliament Hill and Tower alignment is to be viewed with the face towards France.

The measure 72° 30′ less one degree would be Spica, 1950 B.C.; and plus one degree, Antares, 2000 B.C. The exact complement of that measure is 17° 30′, which, like 19° 15′ and 21°, indicate Arcturus with perhaps more height of hill than what I have assumed. The measure 9° 15′ seems to have the same meaning, the complement of which, not otherwise given, 80° 45′, less one degree, would be the Pleiades, 1850 B.C. The mean of the three star-dates would be 1933 B.C.

The measure 76° 45′, less one degree, would be the Pleiades and Spica in 1550 B.C. The complement of 21°, 69°+1°, would be Antares in 1500 B.C. The measure 2° is evidently the complement of 91°=89° twice given, the latter indicating Betelgeuse in 1500 B.C. The measure 28°—1° would be Capella in 1500 B.C. The measure 55° is a multiple of 27° 30′, the complement of which, 62° 30′, is represented in 60° 45′, with some height in the south-east, which indicates Sirius about 1500, warning the August festival. We have here a remarkably strong group of stellar indications, the mean of the five dates being roughly 1500 B.C. We have probably three distinct periods, 3200, 1900 and 1500, the first being the earliest mound date I have been able to make out; the second may be considered as marking the dawn of the Bronze Age in the district; and the third brings us to the period when the whole country was dotted with round mounds or cairns, generally of small dimensions.

In the absence of height measures the dates I have given can only be approximations. For the period 1500 B.C., the agreement of the dates, together with the certainty, I may say, that all the stars indicated were highly honoured, is a striking fact. Dates set aside altogether, the categorical harmony of the measures is certainly evidence of design. Why should the same measures, differing but seldom over one degree, turn up everywhere in the same latitude? If the answer I have given cannot be accepted, the question remains as by far the most important one to be dealt with in connexion with the monuments.

To anticipate one obvious criticism of these remarks, I should say that though the measures themselves, as solar ones, change but little in a thousand years, and that the apparent change is often due to local skyline conditions, and at best difficult to time I have assumed that the actual alignments set up were directed to stars which rose or set in positions which harmonized, and often coincided, with solar positions. It is a star that is to be looked for in each case. The solstitial amplitude is nearly always indicated to within narrow limits, and an agreement of stellar dates within those limits is, in my opinion, first-class evidence.

APPENDIX B

THE ROADS OF GREATER LONDON

MOUNDS and straight roads should be studied together. Signal stations preceded long straight roads, and the mound-builders were the pioneers of road-makers. The positions of mounds, individually and relatively, were determined by astronomical requirements. The astronomy of the mounds is now duplicated in related roads.

The general fact of such interrelation of mounds and roads is well established. In the district immediately dominated by London, there are so many long straight roads offering collectively excellent facts of orientation. The antiquity or age of oriented roads may be, speaking generally, more problematical than that of mounds or other ancient works, for the reason that prehistoric mounds are known to have been used as reference points by modern surveyors. Still the orientation facts should lead to a further inquiry into the landmarks which were utilized by the road-makers.

The directions recorded in these notes were made out with the aid of a protractor on that marvel of accuracy, elegance, and cheapness combined, a shilling four-miles-to-an-inch Ordnance sheet, except in one instance where Bacon's map was used. In surveying a new railway mound at Blaencwm, Rhondda, was used as a reference point. In the list of oriented roads I have included three railways, for two reasons, the obvious significance of their orientations, and the remarkable straight lengths of the sections examined. Even if such sections were made without reference to ancient landmarks, the three orientations indicated are the most important for the student of orientation to remember. Where distances are not given it is to be understood that the interrelations of mounds are meant.

Place	Circle	Distance
CLOCK-STAR ALIGNMENTS.		
Windsor–Slough . .	15° 30′ N.E.–S.W. ..	3 miles.
Surbiton–Epsom . .	16° ,, ,, ..	5 ,,
South London–Streatham	16° 15′ ,, ,, ..	2½ ,,
Tothill–Parliament Hill	16° 30′ N.W.–S.E. ..	—
Streatham-Croydon .	18° 15′ ,, ,, ..	4 ,,
RECTANGULAR ALIGNMENTS TO ABOVE.		
Tower–Westminster .	71° 15′ N.E.–S.W. ..	—
Stanway–Lexden . .	72° 45′ ,, ,, ..	2 ,,
Akeman Road (Ayles- bury–Tring) . .	72° 45′ ,, ,, ..	8 ,,
Oxford Street . .	75° ,, ,, ..	?
Chatham–Dunkirk . .	75° N.W.–S.E. ..	22 ,,
Tothill–Tower . .	76° N.E.–S.W. ..	—
Greenwich–Dartford .	77° 30′ N.W.–S.E. ..	9 ,,
SUMMER SOLSTICE AZIMUTHS.		
Tower–Parliament Hill	46° 30′ N.W.–S.E. .. (with height S.E.) ..	—
Seven Sisters Road (Bacon's Map) . .	48° N.E.–S.W. ..	?
Roman Road (Kelve- don–Marks Tey) .	48° 30′ ,, ,, ..	4 ,,
Roman Road, N.E. of Chelmsford . .	51° ,, ,, ..	4 ,,
WINTER SOLSTICE AZIMUTH.		
Watling Street (Rock- cliffe–Little Buckhill).	48° 30′ N.W.–S.E. .. (height S.E. ?)	5 ,,
HALF OF S.S. AMPLITUDE?		
Watling Street (Bushey Heath–Elstree . .	20° 30′ N.E.–S.W. ..	1 ,,
HALF OF W.S. AMPLITUDE?		
Watling Street (Elstree– St. Stephen's) .	21° 15′ N.W.–S.E. ..	7 ,,
TWICE W.S. AMPLITUDE.		
S.W.R. (Farnborough– Basingstoke) . .	81° N.E.–S.W. ..	19 miles.
Stane Street (Dunmow– Braintree) . .	82° 45′ ,, ,, ..	3 ,,
Colchester (Street) .	84° N.W.–S.E. ..	?

Place		Circle		Distance
TWICE S.S. AMPLITUDE.				
Colchester (Street) .	86°	N.E.–S.W. ..		? miles
Bishop's Storford–Takeley . . .	86°	N.W.–S.E. ..		3 ,,
S.E.R. (Tonbridge–Ashford) . . .	86°	,, ,,	..	26 ,,
Westminster–Windsor .	86° 45′ N.E.–S.W. ..			—
AMPLITUDE OF NOVEMBER SUN.				
Watling Street, near St. Albans . . .	27° 45′ N.W.–S.E. ..			3½ ,,
Little Waltham–Gosfield . . .	26° 45′ N.E.–S.W. ..			4 ,,
(with hill elevation both may be May amplitudes).				
MAY AZIMUTH.				
G.W.R. (Maidenhead–Reading) . . .	62° 15′ N.E.–S.W. ..			9 ,,
HALF MAY AZIMUTH.				
Brentwood–Chelmsford (general direction) .	30° 30′	,, ,,	..	10 ,,
Epsom Road . .	32°	,, ,,	..	12 ,,
HALF OF RECTANGULAR ALIGNMENTS MENTIONED.				
Windsor, S.E. road .	35°	N.W.–S.E. ..		?
Watling Street (Edgware Road) . .	37°	,, ,,	..	10 ,,
TWICE MAY AMPLITUDE.				
Romford–Brentwood .	59°	N.E.–S.W. ..		6 ,,
RECTANGLE TO HALF S.S. AMPLITUDE.				
Kensington–Staines .	67° 30′ N.E.–S.W. ..			14 ,,

The categorical agreement of the map measures should be followed up in each case by a study of the local conditions. The local observatory must, and may be discovered. It is the converging points of several orientations. Each of the mounds was such an observatory. The great Epsom road points to the Tower as its observational base, and both the Edgware Road and the road to Staines point to the neighbourhood of Paddington as their common base. The Church of Streatham represents an ancient observatory, as indeed the parish church generally did. Two streets converge there which jointly formed a star-clock.

It is necessary to bear in mind that if a line which joins two mounds, resulting in a road of the same orientation, can be approximately dated, such a date would apply only to one of the mounds, the other mound may be considerably older; and the best way of ascertaining the age of such a line would be by an examination of the dimensions of each mound.

The Tower-Parliament Hill alignment is the earliest of the kind I have made out. There is every reason for supposing that London should have such early monuments. Taking the circumference of the Windsor mound as 600 feet, I find the fundamental measure to be the same as that of the great circle at Avebury, and the date of the latter I have made out to be practically the same as that of the Tower-Parliament Hill alignment. The circumference of the Windsor mound is a little less than one-sixth of that of Avebury, but the fundamental measure is the same, namely, 37° 30', multiplied by 100 at Avebury, hence the hundred stones which once adorned that circle, and multiplied by 16 at Windsor. The Tower (White Mount), Windsor, and the great bank at Avebury, with Silbury Hill perhaps, are great earth monuments which seem to have immediately followed the great stone monuments of the district, and that about 5,000 years ago, Stonehenge being practically unique, as it certainly is in style, as a belated megalithic monument well within the mound period, which may be expressed as 3200-1000 B.C.

AUTHORITIES CONSULTED.

Ab Ithel.
Alford, Dean.
Aubury, J.
Arnold, Matthew.
Barclay.
Bede.
Besant (Sir Walter).
Blight.
Borlase.
Brut-y-Tywysogion.
Barddas.
Camden.
Caxton.
Chronicles:
    Will. of Malmesbury.
    Florence of Worcester.
    Matt. of Westminster.
    Matt. Paris.
    Geoff. of Monmouth.
    John Hardynge.
    Warren.
    Rob: of Gloucester.
    Roger of Wendover.
    Coke (Lord Chief Justice).
Churchill, Sir Winstone.
Cymmrodorian, Soc. Proceed-
    ings.
Cumming, Miss Gordon.
Cambro-Briton.
Cotsworth.
Davies.
Disraeli.
Drayton.
Dugdale.
Freeman.
Fuller.
Gildas.
Giraldus Cambrensis.
Gould, Rev. S. Baring–.
Griffith, Rev. J.

Guest, Lady Charlotte.
Guest, Dr.
Haddan & Stubbs.
Heylyn.
Hoare, Sir R. Colt.
Hollinshed.
Higgins.
Huntingdon, Henry of.
Iolo MS.
Kitchen, Dean.
Knight, Sir C.
Layard, Sir Henry.
Leland.
Lockyer, Sir Norman.
Lukes, C.
Mallory, Sir Thomas.
Marsden, Rev. W.
Montfaucon.
Morgan, Rev. R. W.
Morien.
Müller, Prof. Max.
Myvyrian Archæology.
Nennius.
Nichols, N. G.
Origen.
Rawlinson.
Rees, Thomas.
Rhys, Sir J.
Sayce.
Schliemann.
Stanley, Dean.
Stevens, Dean.
Stowe.
Stubbs (Bishop).
Stukeley.
Tacitus.
Tertullian.
Triads.
Turner, Sharon.

INDEX

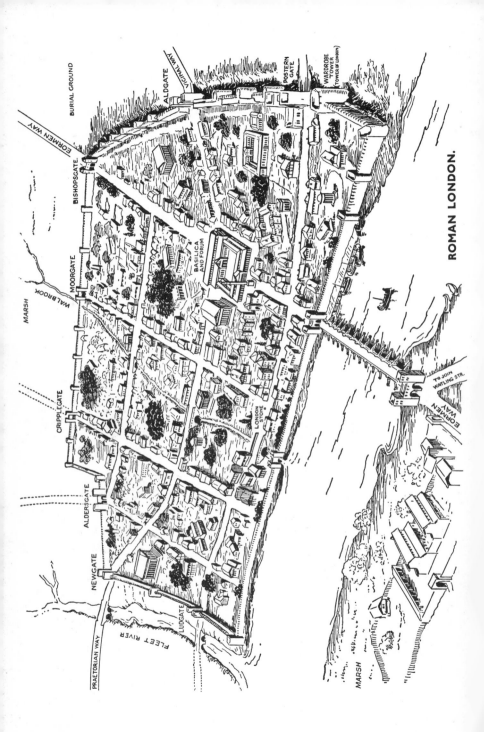

ROMAN LONDON.

BURIAL GROUND

FOSSE WAY

ALDGATE

VICINAL WAY

POSTERN GATE

WARDROBE TOWER (TOWER OF LONDON)

BISHOPSGATE.

MOORGATE

WALBROOK

MARSH

BASILICA AND FORUM

CRIPPLEGATE

ALDERSGATE

LONDON STONE

TO JOIN WATLING STR.

FOSSEN WAY

NEWGATE

LUDGATE

FLEET RIVER

PRAETORIAN WAY

MARSH